Passion for Peonies

PASSION FOR PEONIES

Celebrating the Culture and Conservation of Nichols Arboretum's Beloved Flower

David Michener and Robert Grese, editors

University of Michigan Press • Ann Arbor

Published in the United States of America by the University of Michigan Press
Manufactured in Canada
Printed on acid-free paper

A CIP catalog record for this book is available from the British Library.
Library of Congress Cataloging-in-Publication data has been applied for.

First published May 2020

ISBN: 978-0-472-03780-3 (Paper: alk paper)
ISBN: 978-0-472-12686-6 (ebook)

Contents

APPRECIATING HISTORIC HERBACEOUS PEONIES AND
OTHER HISTORIC GARDEN VARIETIES

PEONIES IN CLASSIC GARDEN WRITING

PEONIES IN ARTS AND CULTURE

Preface

Peonies have long been one of the most beloved garden flowers. With a rich history in Chinese culture, where the parents of many of today's cultivated varieties originated, peonies have developed their own unique history in Western culture as well. They are one of the most popular plants to be passed down through generations in families, with their roots easily divided in late summer. Breeders in Europe and throughout North America have long worked on hybrids for the North American public—with emphases on those with fragrance, unique flower forms, beauty as cut flowers, and forms that hold up well in landscape plantings. Over time, individuals as well as the American Peony Society and the Canadian Peony Society have developed ranking systems for comparing new introductions and old varieties. Many of the highest-ranked and most marketable varieties have survived. Others, developed by individual breeders or for local markets, have largely disappeared. Peony fashions, much like those in the clothing industry, have come and gone over the ages.

This book celebrates the rich cultural history of peonies in North America with stories about key gardens and individuals, representations of peonies in Asian art, and recent scientific research into the genetics and fungal relationships of peonies. It is also a celebration of the one hundredth anniversary of the Peony Garden at Nichols Arboretum in Ann Arbor, Michigan—one of the premier peony gardens in North America and the largest dedicated to historic cultivars. During the past two decades, staff at the arboretum along with an advisory committee of experts have worked to verify the historic cultivars in the garden as a living international reference collection. The garden has become a sacred place for the Ann Arbor community and for the thousands who come to revel in its beauty during the peak bloom time each June.

In addition to telling the story of a magical public space on the University of Michigan campus, this book gathers reprints of seminal historical articles about peonies, essays about key individuals or unique peony gardens, and of course pictures showing the sheer joy of peonies in bloom. Through the chapters and images here, we hope you'll gain a deeper understanding of and appreciation for the rich history of the peony and its role in garden history.

"Still Glorious" by Janet Kohler, courtesy the artist.

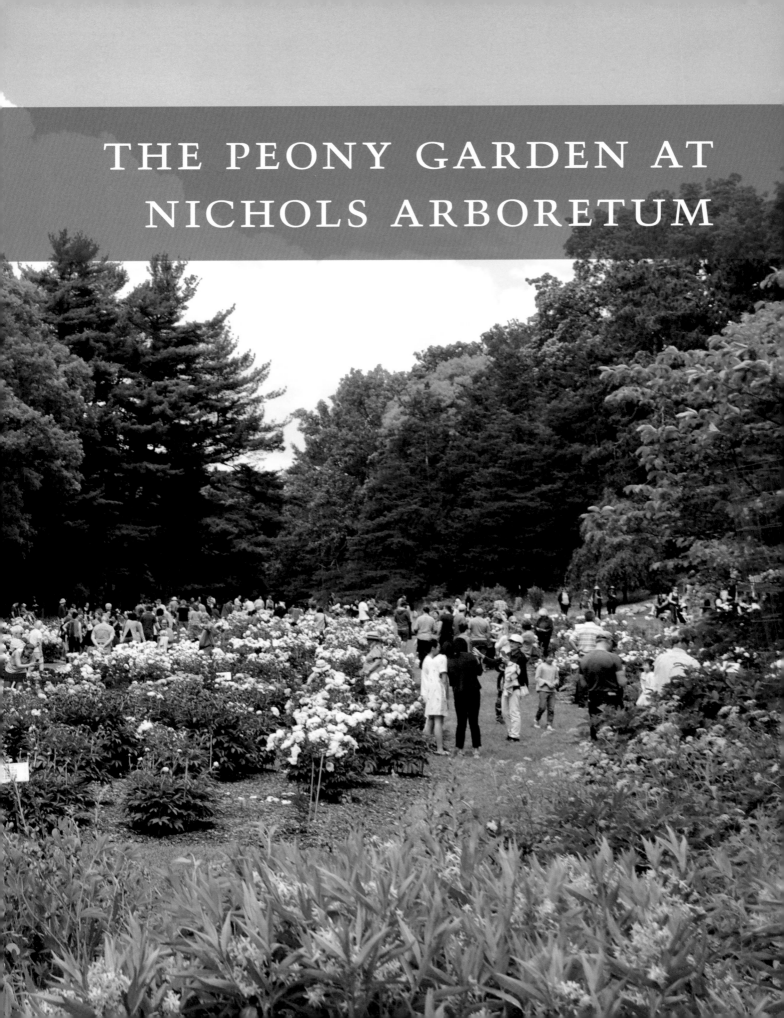

THE PEONY GARDEN AT NICHOLS ARBORETUM

A Century of Blooms

A History of the Peony Garden at Nichols Arboretum

Robert Grese

The Peony Garden at Nichols Arboretum is rooted in the friendship of two men, both peony enthusiasts and both connected to the University of Michigan. One, Aubrey Tealdi, headed both the landscape architecture program at the university as well as Nichols Arboretum. The other, William Erastus (W. E.) Upjohn, was a graduate of the university and the founder of the company that bore his name—the Upjohn Pharmaceutical Company of Kalamazoo, Michigan. Sometime before 1920, they came to know each other, and Upjohn engaged the Italian-born Tealdi to help him create his garden of peonies at his Brook Lodge property, just outside Kalamazoo. Together they developed the idea for a public display garden of peonies at Nichols Arboretum.[1]

Tealdi was born in Florence, Italy around 1881. He studied at the Italian Naval Academy where he gained a thorough knowledge of engineering and spent time in England, where he became familiar with the designs of Capability Brown and Humphrey Repton as well as the writings of William Robinson and Gertrude Jekyll. It's not clear that he ever acquired a professional degree in landscape gardening or architecture. Still, after visiting relatives in Chicago in 1907, he was hired by Ossian Cole Simonds to join his landscape architecture firm.[2]

Simonds had graduated from the University of Michigan with a degree in engineering in 1878, and by 1907 had established a broad-ranging practice throughout the United

William Erastus (W. E.) Upjohn

Aubrey Tealdi

States but with a particular focus on the Midwestern landscape. He is considered to be one of the originators of the "prairie style" of landscape gardening.[3] In 1905, he had been hired by the City of Ann Arbor to lay out several parks and boulevards around the city. He was also hired to design the University of Michigan's botanical garden, a joint project of the city and university, in 1906. While working on those projects, he began giving lectures on landscape design at the university and ultimately convinced the university to establish a program. At Simond's urging, Tealdi was hired as the first instructor in landscape gardening in 1909. Tealdi was assigned responsibility for the former botanical gardens property in 1914 and became director when the property was renamed Nichols Arboretum in 1923.[4] Tealdi was named Professor of Landscape Design in 1919 and served as chair of the program until his retirement in 1934.[5]

W. E. Upjohn, was a graduate of the University of Michigan (1875) and founded the Upjohn Pharmaceutical Company in 1886. The company became known for creating "friable" pills that were easily digested. By the early 1900s he had become a passionate collector and evaluator of herbaceous peonies. Together with Tealdi, he was active in the American Peony Society, serving as treasurer for a term beginning in 1923. Upjohn amassed a renowned collection of peonies at his rural Brook Lodge Estate near Kalamazoo. It held over six hundred cultivars across many acres of display beds. Upjohn enjoyed opening his private collection to the public—free of charge—during the bloom season. He also kept meticulous track of his peonies and privately published the essay "Brook Lodge Gardens—Peonies" (an excerpt is included in this book), which methodically articulates his opinions of their virtues and diverse intriguing facts, peony by peony.

By 1922, Tealdi and Upjohn had decided to create a peony garden at Nichols Arboretum, and Upjohn offered divisions of his peony collection to his alma mater. Upjohn's gift helped to establish one of the most cherished historical collections of peonies anywhere in the United States and Canada. It is enjoyed by thousands of visitors each year when the peonies are in bloom in early June. Many of the cultivars that he and others donated appear in the Peony Garden to this day in the same location they were planted a century ago.

While Tealdi's general approach to garden design tended more to the naturalistic as was the emphasis in O. C. Simonds' office, he chose a strong rectilinear order for the peony garden. Plants were carefully arranged in pairs in ten rows of square beds with fifteen varieties per bed. Each bed was identified by a concrete marker, and visitors were given maps from which they could match each

Red Charm

plant's location to its name and get to know individual cultivars. This system allowed for easy identification without the need for individual plant labels.[6] Tealdi harbored strong democratic notions of garden design, hoping to empower the general public:

> It has been said that landscape gardening is for the rich, but nothing could be more unreasonable than that. Get a B pencil and a rough piece of paper and a $50 Ford and go out and sketch a beautiful picture. It may be the highest kind of art in the results. The same thing is true in gardening. A few packets of seeds and a few plants combined with the feelings which will make a picture, and good hard honest work will get results that money cannot buy.[7]

If creating gardens is a democratic art, peonies are among the most democratic flowers—easily passed down in families and shared among friends. Growing in regions of North America wherever lilacs—among the most treasured woody plants—grow, peonies have

Ann Arbor Observer

May 2014

AnnArborObserver.com

long been one of the most treasured herbaceous flowers. Blooming in mid to late spring, they provide cut flowers for home display and wedding bouquets, for graduation celebrations and other important family events. Until the mid-1960s, when the University of Michigan moved up the date of graduation, peony blooms coincided with the June commencement, adding "a special burst of beauty to the "end-of-school year activities."[8] In June 1935, the *Ann Arbor News* noted that "millions upon millions" of peony flowers were in bloom during June and that they combined to give Ann Arbor "a distinctive charm in the glamorous days, the lingering twilights, and the moon-lit nights of the commencement period."[9]

When the garden officially opened to the public in 1927, the *Ann Arbor News* described the garden as "a riot of color, of crimson, rose and shell pink intermingled with fluffy pompoms of creamy white."[10] The reporter covering the opening had this to say about the garden:

There are peonies such as the amateur gardener dreams of growing but has little hopes of realizing—peonies so large they resemble giant fluff

Facing page: The popular local monthly, the *Ann Arbor Observer,* has used the Peony Garden four times in the last several decades. This cover using a lovely pastel of the garden by Janet Kohler, is from May 2014. Courtesy the *Ann Arbor Observer.*

balls or chrysanthemums of unusual coloring. Solid masses of petals of waxy texture, single blooms resembling huge tulips, others like massive roses, and still others so regular and perfect in formation as to remind one of the old-fashioned flowers that grace mother's hat now reposing in the attic. In fact, there are nearly three hundred varieties represented in the array.[11]

As with many other cities in the Midwest, peonies graced private gardens throughout the city. Two gardens were especially noted for their beauty, and their owners routinely invited the public to come enjoy the peony flowers. Local hardware store owner Andrew Muehlig invited the public to visit his private garden with 372 varieties of peonies. Likewise, construction company owner Carl Weinberg dazzled visitors with 300 varieties and offered a wide variety for sale when the roots were divided each August.[12]

Over the years, the Peony Garden has come to be regarded as a sacred space for the Ann Arbor community, a not-to-be-missed sensation when peonies are in bloom. The rather short period of peak bloom—about two weeks each year—only broadens the appeal of the garden. If you miss the peak bloom time, you have to wait a full year.

During the garden's early years, people were allowed to drive through the arboretum ("the Arb," as locals called it), and callous visitors would drive wherever they wanted, damaging plantings in the process. Surrounding the garden with a chain-link fence and opening it only during bloom time seemed like a logical solution. Climbing roses were planted along the north side of the fence, disguising it and adding another attractive feature to the garden. In this early period, it was open only from two or three in the afternoon until eight at night. After cars were banned throughout Nichols Arboretum, the fence was removed and the pathway through the Peony Garden became a regular entrance for people accessing the arboretum from Washington Heights. After the Burnham House was moved to this location in 1999 and was named the James D. Reader Urban Environmental Education Center, Washington Heights became the official major entrance to Nichols Arboretum.

After 1965, when the university switched to an early May or late April graduation date, the peonies ceased to be associated with graduation time. With students no longer around campus when the peonies came into bloom, the bloom became more of a community than a campus event. After the Friends of Nichols Arboretum was formed in 1991, the group initiated "Peony Parties" each year to coincide with the bloom time. The parties evolved into

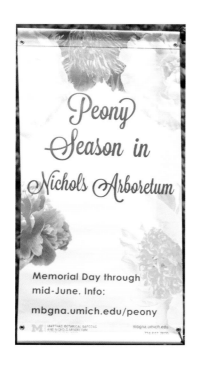

Shakespeare in the Arb, celebrating its twentieth annual production in 2020, coincides with the bloom of peonies in the Peony Garden.

a rollicking festival with music, face painting, peony-themed hats, and refreshments as visitors strolled through the garden admiring the flowers. These art-themed events eventually became known as "Arbfest." Choosing the exact day for the annual party became nerve-racking exercise, and occasionally the date was set too early or too late to catch the peonies at their peak. In more recent years, Nichols Arboretum staff have planned a series of events over the bloom period so at least some of them fall near the peak bloom time. The schedule has included a concert of Chinese-themed flower music called "Peony Blossoms and Pure Melodies," originally in collaboration with the Confucius Institute at the university and meant to honor the Asian origin of most peonies.

Since 2000, the bloom time has coincided with the annual production of Shakespeare in the Arb, a collaboration with the university's Residential College. The first of these plays was *A Midsummer Night's Dream*, which now rotates with other Shakespeare plays. These are environmental productions—the audience moves through the Arb with the actors, transforming the

landscape into a magical kingdom. Many of the plays have begun in the Peony Garden, using the colorful blooms as a backdrop. Others use the garden as an entrance to the different settings in the arboretum where the play is staged.

While the peonies are in bloom, the garden becomes a delightful setting for watching the pure joy people feel when they visit. Some come dressed to the hilt, while others stop by on a casual run through the Arb. The garden is a popular place for wedding photos and families who come to pose young children against the backdrop of riotous color. In recent years, the ability to take casual shots with smartphones has greatly expanded photography in the garden. Visitors are as likely to see the blooms through a screen as look with the naked eye. People record their favorite flowers or take selfies to share with their friends. Others come to the garden merely to relax.

Patients, their families, and medical staff take breaks in the garden as respite from stresses in nearby hospitals. I've had people point to the hospital and note that that's where they go for treatments, but the Arb, they say, is where they come for therapy. A case in point is the story of Ginger (Visel) Ford who contracted polio in the winter of 1950 and was forced to go through regular outpatient treatments at the University of Michigan's Bone and Joint Clinic. After one of her sessions, Ginger's Mom took her over to the Peony Garden, and she discovered a true sense of peace among the mesmerizing blooms. The Peony Garden continued to be Ginger's "happy place" where she brought her own children years later.[13]

When Dr. Upjohn's original gift was accepted by the university's regents, they appropriated $2,000 for the establishment of the garden and $500 for its care during that first year.[14] Tealdi's geometric design of the garden provided for about four hundred varieties, with two specimens of each. The initial emphasis was on herbaceous peonies, with the intention to add tree peonies on the slope above the garden.[15] When the garden was officially opened to the public in 1927, the Regents appropriated another $250 for a celebration.[16]

Tealdi sought to showcase peonies of known merit, with advice and input not only from Dr. Upjohn, but also from other peony experts and growers, among them A. M. Brand of Faribault, Minnesota (featured later in this book); L. R. Bonnewitz from Van Wert, Ohio; E. C. Shaw; T. C. Thurlow's Sons of West Newbury, Massachusetts; Judge Vories from St. Joseph, Missouri; and Northbrook Gardens of Northbrook, Illinois. He also received donations and advice from local experts such as Andrew Muehlig. Tealdi wrote an article in the *American Peony Society Bulletin* in 1929 describing the establishment of the garden and in 1931 published

Nawal Motawi created historically inspired tile in her garage before forming Motawi Tileworks in 1992, now a multimillion-dollar venture.

Motawi Tileworks' 4" x 8" Peony, available in pale blue and red, is a favorite among local visitors. Motawi spent hours adapting the design for ceramic. The result of the intricate process: a work of art befitting Motawi's beloved garden flower, although she wishes it could capture that scent!

a second article, noting varieties he desired to add and asking members of the American Peony Society to donate roots.[17]

Over the history of the Peony Garden, caring for it has fluctuated with the budget available at the arboretum and the priorities of its director and staff. As a collection of herbaceous plants, the Peony Garden has always been somewhat of an anomaly at the arboretum, with its focus on woody plants and natural woodlands. Peony gardens at several other colleges and universities have fared poorly over time. Cornell's extensive peony collection has greatly decreased, while the once-extensive collection at the University of Illinois has disappeared completely. Swarthmore's garden of both tree and herbaceous peonies is now focused primarily on tree peonies.

In 2008 the Peony Garden initiative began, an effort to fully document the collection as a reference garden, preserve historic varieties for the future, and raise endowment funds to care for the garden. A group of international advisers from the American Peony Society and the Canadian Peony Society joined with Nichols Arboretum staff to verify the identification of each peony in the garden. Whereas the vision by Tealdi and Upjohn was that the garden would continue to evolve, featuring newly developing peonies and older varieties would be discarded, the current vision of the garden is as a reference collection of historic cultivars.

What exactly is a *cultivar*? A *cultivar* is a cultivated variety or named selection of a plant. The precision of the term has changed as biology, genetics, and patent law have developed. Modern cultivars are genetically identical. These are clones of one mother plant. Peony cultivars introduced years ago were usually clones but some may be from sibling seeds of a particular hybrid cross. Many if not most of the breeders included in this book deliberately crossed different cultivars to create the new varieties they introduced.

The Peony Garden has become a nationally accredited collection under the American Public Gardens Association and has backed up many of its most rare varieties at other gardens throughout the United States and Canada. Today, it is the largest collection of historic peony varieties in North America, with target dates of varieties introduced before 1950.

Now approaching its centennial, the Peony Garden of Nichols Arboretum remains one of the most cherished gardens in North America and serves as a reference for other peony gardens everywhere. For visitors each June, it provides a place to be immersed in the mingling colors and fragrances of the flowers. For a while, time is suspended, and you can forget about anything else.

Montreal Botanical Garden

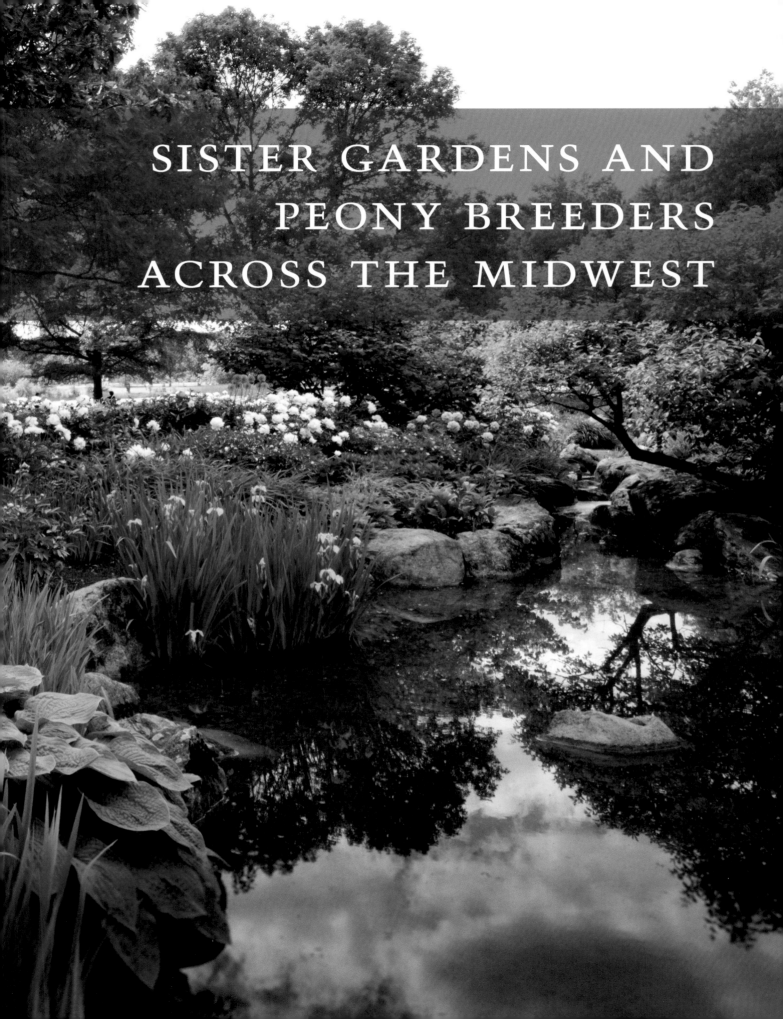

SISTER GARDENS AND
PEONY BREEDERS
ACROSS THE MIDWEST

Brook Lodge Gardens —Peonies

W. E. Upjohn
with Commentary by David Michener

In the evolution of human industrial achievements our success has been so great as to inject a new problem in our social affairs. While sixteen hours a day fifty years ago was scarcely adequate to produce the necessities of life, though the requirements of those days were meager compared with today's extravagant demands, still eight hours today threatens the production of more than our distributive schemes will require. This difference of time is our problem; the added leisure is already hazarding our morals. The sociologist may have his answer, the moralist his. We who are lovers of flowers should add our contribution.

The human heart aspires to the mountain tops. Our souls demand the moments of exaltation. Of the human joys, the joy of beauty is the one most universally demanded and gives the most universal satisfaction. The joy of the mate may die with satiety, the satisfaction of the love for the beautiful may be as evanescent but it is also perennial so an extension of the appreciation of flowers is a social necessity. The choice of a flower is a personal matter. If the rose lifts you to the upper levels, grow roses. If the daffodil gives you greatest joy because it is the flower of budding spring, grow daffodils. If the gods have sent Juno's messenger to introduce to you the celestial blue of the iris and you are enamored of it, then grow iris. They are of so many forms and so great beauty. If the modern fad has struck home and the gladiolus has obsessed you, wait for the gladiolus for your special satisfaction. But in all your hunting after the good, don't overlook the best, the peony, that one great flower in its many forms all so different and so lovely, the one flower which commands your attention every month in the year.

Dr. W. E. Upjohn's privately published booklet, *Brook Lodge Gardens–Peonies*, captures both his confident voice and distinctive perspective. Published before 1927, its 153 entries are far more than just an alphabetical listing of his favorite peonies—together they present a compelling and coherent concept of perfection in floral beauty. His opening sentence, a riveting thunderbolt on moral hazard, sets the tone: "In the evolution of human industrial achievements our success has been so great as to inject a new problem in our social affairs." His is an epistle addressing all who do and should love peonies, then flowing into an annotated roll-call of (with exceptions that prove the rule) virtuous peonies. Who knew until that moment that our cultivating peonies was an inoculant from moral degeneracy? His notes convey what his experienced eye appreciated as upholding enduring values by which newer cultivars could, and must, not only be assessed but judged. His notes guide new peony lovers toward thrifty decisions rather than being misled by inflamed marketing as well as the trap of irresponsibly high prices. His corporation's motto 'Keep the Quality Up' appears to be a declaration for his appreciation of peonies, too. [The entire booklet is available as a free pdf from the Peony Garden website as well as https://www.biodiversitylibrary.org/item/237871#page/1/mode/1up]

Dr. Upjohn captured the pinnacle of "lactiflora" peony appreciation in North America, just before the herbaceous hybrid peonies became the rage. These hybrids often have a 'lacti' as a parent, and are the most commonly seen peonies in North America today. However, then and even more-so-now, these historic 'lactiflora' cultivars were treasured for their heady fragrances unlike any others in the floral realm, their nuanced colors from white to deep red, and their sensuous transformation from alluring buds into voluptuous floral beauties. As you read his notes, recall that unknown to Dr. Upjohn, public appreciation of his beloved treasury would undergo a sea-change where hybrids with bolder-colored and sometimes simpler flowers on stronger stems captured the public's fancy, but, alas, often at the expense of fragrance.

Quality must not be confused with price or force of marketing. 'Coronne d'Or' is recommended because "the price is low. They are not cheap." By contrast, 'Gismonda' "will be better known when the price is lower." Upjohn appreciated that many gardeners had quite limited budgets and were needing multiple plants for their own needs (including local sales) so 'Karl Rosenfield's note of being a

enthusiasm for them is what has kept her mentally keen, notwithstanding her ninety years then we should all grow peonies. She thinks this one is one of her best. It is an enormous flat rose type of a true but a light rose color. We have too few rose tints.

Festiva Maxima (Miallez 1851)

9.3 (84) Early

Like old furniture old flowers are kept in fashion because they are good, and not because they are old. Festiva Maxima has its virtues beyond the most and should be largely used because of its price. It lacks some of the charm of some of the newer whites which are not marred by the crimson fleckings. However, some like these contrasts and the Festivas (both) should be enticing to those who like this sign of blood and breeding. Coming early it has much competition from which comparative selections can be made. A large flower, strong habit and a fair keeper.

Henry Avery

Henry Avery (Brand 1907)

8.5 (16) Late

It may be we did not get a true Henry Avery. Certainly we did not get a white Henry Avery. Perhaps Mr. Brand is again calling pink, white. Ours is a soft pink flower of rose type. Altogether a good plant. A fragrant bloom coming late.

Jubilee

Jubilee (Pleas 1908)

8.9 (38) Midseason

An extremely large very flat flower of the rose type. A white peony with warmer tints when first opening. With its narrow informal petals it is an attractive flower. It is a pity it did not inherit stronger stems, still it is distinctive and desirable. Midseason.

Mme Emile Galle (Crousse 1881)

8.5 (65) Late

Another piece of old furniture. Shell pink flowers on long stems, rather weak but sufficient. When such flowers as these are planted, popularity of the peony is increased.

Mme Emile Galle

Marguerite Gerard

Karl Rosefield

Lady Alexandra Duff

Marguerite Gerard (Crousse 1892)

8.4 (56) Late

It is always a pleasure to let your enthusiasm run riot in describing a flower of the quality of Marguerite Gerard. In the language of the census man the subject is a female, belongs to the white race of the voluptuous type of beauty—the blushing bride among peonies. Strong grower, free bloomer, tall and late.

Karl Rosefield (Rosefield 1908)

8.8 (57) Midseason

Karl Rosefield and Richard Carvel are two of the outstanding reds among peonies. Rosefield is a brilliant dark crimson of extremely good substance and form. A thrifty grower and a good divider. Keeps well as a cut flower.

Kelway's Glorious (Kelway 1909)

9.8 (33) Late midseason

The steadily maintained high price of this plant reflects its universally accepted value. A most glorious flower on a plant of good habit but of a rather slow growth. Not at its best until the fourth year. An immense white flower of the greatest purity. Very fragrant.

Lady Alexandra Duff (Kelway)

9.1 (49) Early midseason

An over advertised, still an attractive flower if one is fortunate enough to procure a good strain. A large cup-shaped flower of rose type with wide delicately pink petals. Free bloomer, robust habit. Very fragrant.

Le Cygne (Lemoine 1907)

9.9 (56) Midseason

The rating of this flower shows the place it holds in the hearts of peony lovers, having but one competitor for this rating. When the stock permits an attractive price everyone will want it. A milk white globe of immense size and great beauty.

Marie Crousse (Crousse 1892)

8.9 (50) Late midseason

Large bloom of the bomb type. Shell pink of delicate coloring. A very attractive fragrant flower borne on stiff upright stems. From midseason to late. Looks better than it sounds.

Primevere (Lemonine 1907)

8.6 (47) Midseason

Like the search for the Holy Grail the search for the yellow peony has not been completely successful. However, Primevere is somewhat yellow in color and moreover a most charming flower. One of the sweetest of odors and a good keeper as a cut flower.

Therese (Dessert 1904)

9.8 (71) Midseason

It is impossible to say anything against Therese and equally impossible to say anything which has not been said in her praise. We could wish however, that they had left out some of the blueing when she was laundered and we could also have wished that she had been made a little less large or that her mother had given her more strength to make this size more virile. Altogether a good flower. Reminds one of a loose butterfly not far from the chrysalis state. Midseason.

Triomphe de l'Exposition de Lille (Calot 1865)

7.8 (42) Late midseason

This long and not lovely name would have discouraged a flower of less worth. It is good and when not in competition with better pink peonies it is satisfying. Light shell pink splashed with rose. Quite as attractive as Asa Gray. Late midseason.

Marie Crousse

Primevere

Therese

Silvia Saunders

Silvia Saunders

Positioning Hybrid Peonies for Public Acceptance

David Michener

That's 'Silvia Saunders'—I haven't seen her in *years!*" roared Don Hollingsworth in front of an unidentified specimen in our Peony Garden. He seemed as delighted as if he'd entered a fiftieth class reunion and spotted a classmate who hadn't aged a day. And he was incredulous that we had inventoried such a distinctive peony as unknown. We certainly knew it wasn't anything common.

Silvia Saunders (1901–1994), the person for whom this peony was named, was as influential in the pivotal changes sweeping the peony world in the mid-twentieth century as she was unheralded. She appears to have been as precise, decisive, and resolute in her work as her fabled father, Professor A. P. Saunders, known as the father of modern hybrid peonies. In 1921 he named this elegantly simple peony for his daughter. It's a pinnacle of his early work with the common *lactiflora* peony before he started his epochal interspecies hybridizing program. The single to slightly doubled flowers of 'Silvia Saunders' (*facing page*) open as slightly cupped, light pink chalices, and then fade to white, with all the tonal gradations being attractive. When the side buds are left on, they come into bloom before the top flower passes, creating entire branches that by themselves are delightful bouquets. But florists do not want side flowers: they appropriate nutrients that would otherwise enlarge the top flower. 'Silvia Saunders' was a dud in the commercial market and soon was nearly extinct.

Once our 'Silvia Saunders' was recovered from inventory amnesia, we reached out to colleagues at Winterthur Museum, Garden and Library, and then Hamilton College, in Clinton, New York, to place her in context.

Requiem

Postilion

At Winterthur, once the estate of H. F. du Pont, correspondence with the Saunders family runs deep.[1] It began with a simple road trip in 1946, when du Pont traveled to Clinton, where his wife's cousin, Mrs. Elihu Root, was a noted gardener and the family well established (Elihu Root was awarded the Nobel Peace Prize in 1913, among other distinctions) and close friends of Professor Saunders, who was on the faculty of Hamilton College. In that visit began a lifelong band of friendships that changed how hybrid peonies are accepted. Du Pont spent hours that day in the peony fields, became a passionate devotee of Professor Saunders's hybrid peonies, and soon ordered thirty-two of them. He decided to have the site of his former iris garden at his already fabled Winterthur reconceived by landscape architect Marian Coffin as a peony garden dedicated to Saunders's peonies. It is so to this day, as is the Root Garden at Hamilton College.[2] Both Professor and Miss Saunders—by then they ran the family peony business together—consulted with du Pont on this garden, and likely from that first visit. After Professor Saunders's death, du Pont maintained a "flood of letters" with Silvia for the rest of his life. Not surprisingly, 'Silvia Saunders' was included among the peonies planted at Winterthur. This specimen did not survive the intervening decades, so Linda Eirhart, director of horticulture at Winterthur, asked for a division, which was delivered the next fall. Thus 'Silvia Saunders' lives on in two historic peony collections.

Remarkable as the outcome of that fortuitous road trip was, one could not anticipate the revolutionary next chapter. Silvia Saunders understood intense research and preparation (both parents were academics: her mother had a PhD in English from Bryn Mawr in 1897), and after graduating from Radcliffe began a career in commercial art and photography in New York: the essence of marketing via image.[3] These skills were applied years later while running the family peony nursery. Her father's modern hybrid peonies were treasured among peony specialists but needed to break through into the highest levels of international horticulture and media acclaim. One senses in Silvia Saunders an astute, opinionated businesswoman at the intersection of connoisseurship and contemporary aesthetics. By February 1962, Silvia, Grace Root (Elihu's daughter-in-law), and H. F. du Pont were planning an audacious quest. Their thunderbolt would come out of the clear sky—a stunning exhibit at the 1962 Chelsea Flower Show—and thereby reposition Saunders's peonies in the gardening world. The logistics alone would be as breathtaking as the budget would be steep. It would require collecting at least four hundred of Saunders's hybrid peony buds in gardens in the United States in the first two weeks of May. Each would be individually wrapped and brought to

Coralie

New York and then flown—refrigerated—to London, with Silvia Saunders escorting. Once through customs and to Chelsea, they would be staged by Saunders as an entire exhibit, a scene preplanned in detail with du Pont but adjusted under intense time-pressure to the realities of how the buds traveled, for some would certainly fail. The electrifying thunderbolt would be the buds unfurling at the perfect moment for judging, with the ensuing frenzied attention. Silvia telegraphed du Pont in anticipation: "I wonder if you would think it wise to notify the New York Times of our coming Exhibition . . . we could arrange to cable the Times . . . if we win any awards."

What a thunderbolt it was—for they won not one award, but several! In a letter she informed her nursery's followers of the trove: "the Lindley Silver Medal for Exhibits of Special Interest," followed by a list of individual floral awards. Her letter ends, "All in all, it was a very beautiful Exhibit—certainly the finest that I have ever had a hand in. I know you will all be happy about it, and especially for my father," who had died in 1953. They had rocketed Saunders's hybrid peonies onto the world stage.

Silvia's work in prompting hybrid peonies did not end there. Noted peony breeder Bill Seidl (1932–2016) (some of his selections are in the Intersectional Bed of the Peony Garden) recounted that at his first national peony show in 1968, a sweet elder lady—he knew immediately it was Silvia Saunders—encouraged him.[4] She took extensive time introducing him to key peony breeders. During her tenure as president of the American Peony Society (1968–70) she organized an annual workshop for peony breeders and until her death challenged everyone with her ideas of what was yet missing that new hybrids could produce.[5]

Athena

Edward Auten Jr.

Peonies That Are Different

David Michener

Edward Auten Jr. of Princeville, Illinois, was among the most prolific peony breeders in US history, having introduced at least 297 cultivars from his nursery. A good number of his selections remain popular today, and some of his best are distinctive gems in the Peony Garden in Nichols Arboretum. Yet today he is almost unknown outside a small circle of peony connoisseurs and historians.[1] Auten was active in several professional societies, including the American Peony Society, but my focus is on how his peonies both broadened the public's aspirations for superior peonies and captured the zeitgeist of the era in which the Peony Garden was established.

Peonies enthralled Auten by 1910, since in 1926 he acknowledged sixteen years of "critical experience with fine peonies."[2] By then he had become a self-described "country banker," his success in part due to his local roots. Born in Princeville in 1881, he returned after graduating from Harvard with a degree in economics and music, Class of 1904, joining his father's firm, Auten & Auten, as a banker and cashier. At first he devoted himself to family, church organ, choir, and local politics—not a peep about peonies is noted in the reports to Harvard's secretary.[3]

Something must have happened to this civic-centered man. A turning point may have been when his effort to work with breeding roses was terminated by the severe winter of 1909. He expressed a "deep interest" in working with peonies to develop and commercialize "an improvement or something quite different," the fruits of which put Princeville on the map. Eventually visitors would flock from across the nation, even internationally, to see his fields and trial areas in bloom. From this "laboratory," as he called his peony fields, he selected and trialed hundreds of seedlings, culling them to concentrate on the superior ones. As his passion for peonies grew, so did the acreage that he devoted to the plants. Over time, the work increased such that he had several assistants until well after the Second World War.[4]

There is no doubt that in peonies Auten loved both novel floral innovations and everything red—as deep, and with as little purple undertone, as possible. His quest for perfection in elevating structural elegance with saturated red has given us a beloved legacy in 'Chocolate Soldier', 'John Harvard', and 'Sword Dance'. But he was open to exceptions to the main trajectory of his work, as demonstrated by his "novelty shades," which ranged from "delicate peach pink" in 'Shy Maid' to the "deep angry cerise" in 'High Jinks'. One can only wonder what he would have accomplished with roses had he lived in a slightly warmer clime.

Perfection in "Japanese" peonies became his passion. This floral form, commonly shortened to "Japs," was developed in Japan centuries ago, but only became known in the West during the late 1800s. It is a distinctive and often stunningly beautiful floral form in which stamens, the parts with the pollen-bearing anthers, are partially transformed to petal-like structures. These "petaloids" may look much like stamens or become curved or twisted, and often have the color of the petals. Auten was so respected in his development of "Japs" that when faculty at the University of Illinois developed the Trial Garden there for the commercial development of single and Japanese peonies, Auten was one of the representatives consulted.[5]

Competition engaged Auten, and he wrote confidently both in and out of the winner's role. In his 1929 catalog, he highlighted which of his peonies won national awards from the American Peony Society during 1925–27 and stated that some of his best selections had not yet made it to the national show for judging. Ever the good businessman, he then listed his winners with new and mostly reduced pricing. By 1934 he boasted that "Auten originations have won more official awards from the Seedling Committee of the American Peony Society than those of any grower."

One distinctive angle of Auten's work with peonies was his consistent pride and vigor in marketing a selection of seedlings that were not quite up to his personal standards. These "seedlings" were not what we mean in common English in reference to marigolds, tomatoes, or even young plants. Here *seedling* is a term for peonies that are proven to be of a great floral distinction but not the highest category for the breeder to name and market immediately. These superior but unnamed plants Auten promoted as an opportunity

Preceding page: Auten remains fabled for his many red "Japanese" peonies. Our venerable specimen listed as 'Nippon Beauty' is a fine example.

Auten with 'Do Tell', one of his most famous peonies, and still widely available. Courtesy Princeville Heritage Museum, Princeville, IL.

for the homeowner to purchase a peony unlike any other—with the prerogative of giving it a name that would start one's own "pass along" living family legacy: "I have worked out a new scheme of selling peonies, and I believe I am the first originator and hybridizer to offer you in peonies what you get from an oil painting, from the Paris dressmaker, when you buy a new creation . . . from the master jeweler[,] when you buy a hand wrought silverware or unique setting for a precious stone." He was promoting individuality—a core element of the American psyche. By 1934, with the country in the throes of the Great Depression, he was promoting individual seedlings of known color at one price range, as well as massed lots of one hundred with an enticing unit pricing. One lasting significance

Early Scout

of this practice of selling unnamed but hardly inferior seedlings is that many must have been siblings of the champions he did prize enough to name. While this practice certainly promoted the distribution of Auten's peony lines, the enduring consequence is that look-alikes, as in old cemeteries and homesteads, must be both common and viewed as "from Auten" rather than as unambiguously one of his prized named selections. Only genomic tools will allow their true relationships to be affirmed.[6]

Once we are past their sheer beauty, a striking aspect of Auten's peonies is their evocative names. Unlike many of his contemporaries, Auten named very few for specific women, family members, chums and colleagues, or friends of either gender. Instead, Auten used names that captured the imagination of the rising middle class. Names from everyday speech. Names that resonated and give us a glimpse into the heartland's spirit.

Over thirty peonies' names create a roll call of hardworking American towns and places that were the bedrock of early twentieth-century prosperity and the civic life these towns fostered. By its name each was celebrated, and he emphasized his native Midwest.

Chocolate Soldier

Peonies of distinctive red, mulberry pink, or white honored such towns as Calumet, Creve Coeur, Dearborn (Illinois, not Michigan— Auten emphasized places "of the great Illinois river to Lake Michigan thoroughfare"), Galena, Hennepin . . . all the way to Valencia, Vandalia, and Vincennes. Another set of names suggests themes in magic and fantasy, perhaps reflecting the role of the traveling shows that were so important in the life of the towns and small cities he knew so well.

An assemblage of peonies salute an early Americana patriotic spirit—a sentiment very much in keeping with popular music after the First World War. Here we find almost twenty examples that are usually red flowered, including 'Beacon Hill', 'Betsy Ross' (double white), 'Daniel Boone', 'Drummer Boy', 'Explorer', 'Molly Pitcher', 'Molly Stark' (both Mollys are pink), 'Paul Revere', 'Puritan Maid' (a single white), and 'Town Crier'. Absent are names evoking the Civil War—although some of its veterans would have been alive during his childhood.

Tribal and First Nations names form a notable set of red peonies.

A few are also place-names: 'Arapahoe' (originally 'Aztec'), 'Black Hawk', 'Chieftain', 'Dakota', 'Illini', 'Iroquois', 'Kahokia' . . . through 'Sun Dance', 'Thunderbird', and 'War Hawk'. To my knowledge these names carried no obvious pejorative meaning. It seems likely Auten was using a vernacular association of "Indians" with "red" to convey a color expectation.

More problematic are the peony names evoking African American stereotypes. Although there are only nine in this set, they are pejorative, reflecting an era when African American associations evoked well-known tropes nationwide, Jim Crow laws were becoming well-established norms, the KKK was expanding into the Midwest, and the race riot in Tulsa, Oklahoma, was in recent memory. My sense is Auten had a nuanced ear for the emotional power of American vernacular and used these potent names to convey that these peonies were as dark as could be. This vocabulary communicated as none other. I originally thought 'Chocolate Soldier' was respectful,[7] but have since learned it is rooted in a stock character and song from popular music. By Auten's time it was also used to signify African American enlisted men, and depending on context, not positively. 'Dusty Dinah', 'Minstrel Boy', 'Sambo','Tar Baby', 'Uncle Remus', and 'Uncle Tom' are still recognizable and fraught with meaning. 'Zip Coon' was a blackface minstrel character as well as the title of another vaudeville song (Auten was evidently familiar with popular music), while 'Zulu Bride' likely refers to a krewe role in New Orleans's Mardi Gras. In his era, the role was played by men.

All these were lustrously dark-red peonies—a color that was and remains Auten's signature, as seen in the still popular 'Chocolate Soldier', 'John Harvard', and 'Sword Dance'. Other than 'Chocolate Soldier', none of the pejoratively-named peonies are in the trade or in known peony collections. All are now sought after by a small set of cultural historians, including in African American museum contexts.

As a banker recorded in trade publications, Auten traveled throughout the region, so it is noteworthy that none of his banking contemporaries are honored with peony names. The sole banking name appears to be Tonti, which honors either Lorenzo de Tonti or his sons. Tonti was the originator of the tontine investment system in the seventeenth century, which was still used in the nineteenth century for raising capital. One son was a founder of Detroit; the other was an expeditionary associate of La Salle and assigned to hold Fort Crevecoeur in Illinois while La Salle returned to Canada—

Auten's peony fields were dynamic, unlike a display garden. Plants had to earn their keep—notice the partially empty rows as well as rows full of plants ready for the next sales season. Courtesy Princeville Heritage Museum, Princeville, IL.

returning us to Auten's familiarity with and love for the American heartland. Perhaps all are being honored!

Dramatically different red peonies were Auten's point of pride and are the core of his legacy. By 1934 his catalog featured not just reds, but *categories of reds*. The main listing begins with his "Highest Rated Red Peony," his 'Nippon Beauty', followed by "Auten Standard Red Japs," with fifteen cultivars, "Auten Standard Red Singles," with nineteen cultivars, "Auten Standard Red Semi-Doubles," with nine cultivars, and "Auten Double Reds for the Cut Flower Trade," with three cultivars.

Perhaps the greatest wonder from Auten's hands, and his favorite, was 'Do Tell', an exquisite pinnacle of peony breeding and still popular. The irony? It is not red at all. But it is the acme of both his career and his aspiration: an improvement and something quite different.

Peony field in Van Wert, Ohio

Mrs. Sarah A. Pleas

Hidden in Plain Sight

David Michener

Who was Mrs. Pleas of Indiana? She burst upon the peony world in 1916 when the *New York Times* carried the news that her 'Jubilee' won Best of Show, while duly noting she was nearly ninety years old. 'Jubilee' would triumph for years at flower shows, in part due to the efforts of businessman and promoter Lee Bonnewitz of Van Wert, Ohio, who traveled to shows with it. He wanted the world to be in awe of this fine peony, as well as (no doubt) to encourage people to purchase plants from nurseries around Van Wert.[1] Thus when the annual Van Wert Peony Festival began in 1932, 'Jubilee' was the obvious floral icon, and has remained so ever since.[2]

Behind the shadow of her own fabulous peony, Mrs. (it seemed to always be Mrs.) Sarah Pleas introduced more than fifty peonies under her own name. She was reported to have bred many more that were named by the commercial nurserymen who distributed her cultivars across the decades. The scant historical record indicates that she first planted peony seedlings in 1855, the year after she married Elwood Pleas. This was early in American peony breeding,[3] and it is not clear which peonies she would have been using. In 1897 Elwood died. In 1905 another Van Wert peony grower, a Mr. Anderson, visited and procured one of her newest: 'Jubilee'. She had only recently started using her name as the breeder, and this peony was special. She had named it in honor of what would have been her and Elwood's wedding jubilee. Not long after, she moved to California. There is no doubt Elwood was central to her life: she wrote a twelve-stanza poem, "The Quest of Love," revealing to the reader how her 'Elwood Pleas' peony came to be.[4]

Mrs. Pleas and her peony introductions were so important to Dr. W. E. Upjohn, visionary of the Peony Garden, that not only did he

Dr. Upjohn valued Pleas' peonies as cut flowers. This arrangement shows that peony flowers as well as opening buds were esteemed. Courtesy Donald Reid Parfet / The Upjohn Company Collection. Privately held. Kalamazoo, MI.

prize some of her specimens, but he made a point to track her down for a conversation. Of 'Elwood Pleas' he penned: "It was my pleasure in 1922 to visit that fine character who produced this peony, Mrs. Pleas, then and perhaps now, living in Whittier, California. If the growing of peonies and an intense enthusiasm for them is what has kept her mentally keen, notwithstanding her ninety years then we should all grow peonies. She thinks this one is one of her best."[5]

Today, the Peony Garden has its original 'Jubilee', almost certainly from Dr. Upjohn.[6] As noted by all who have grown this cultivar, including Dr. Upjohn, its stems are too weak to hold the massive flower aloft. But what a beauty it is. The garden also has Pleas's 'Opal', again via Dr. Upjohn. The quest to replace for our long-missing 'Elwood Pleas' continues. As with others of hers lost to time, 'Elwood Pleas' is likely hidden in plain sight, a bit like Mrs. Pleas herself, in the pool of romance-laden peonies blooming every spring in historic parks and cemeteries across our region.[7]

Amateur Breeders and Peony Enthusiasts

Robert Grese

Throughout the country, but particularly in the Midwest, amateur peony enthusiasts and breeders created large gardens and collections. Of the many varieties created by these enthusiasts, few made it into the nursery trade and survive today. Most had passing local interest and then disappeared.

Ann Arbor, Michigan, may have been somewhat typical in terms of local enthusiasts. While the University of Michigan's Peony Garden at Nichols Arboretum took center stage during peony bloom time after it opened in 1927, two local enthusiasts opened their gardens to the public while their peonies were in bloom. Andrew Muehlig, whose family ran a local funeral home, also owned one of the dominant hardware stores downtown.[1] He was active in a variety of community groups, including serving as president of the park commission. At his home just north of downtown, he established a large private garden that he opened to the public during peony bloom season. His garden was noted for its collection of some 372 distinct varieties of herbaceous and tree peonies, including many that were rare. In 1921, A. M. Brand, a grower of peonies for twenty-eight years with over ninety acres of peonies in Fairbault, Minnesota, visited Muehlig's garden.[2]

Another peony enthusiast, Carl Weinberg, the owner of a local construction company, was an amateur breeder and grower and established a large garden of peonies on the west side of Ann Arbor. He routinely advertised peony roots for sale during the months of August and September. It is likely that many of his plants ended up in gardens throughout Ann Arbor. Weinberg's garden was said to contain three hundred varieties and rival the Peony Garden for overall beauty. His collection included an 'Alice Harding' from Nice,

Carl Weinberg's garden on the west side of Ann Arbor where he grew and sold a variety of plants, including peonies. Courtesy Grace Shackman.

Preceding page: Andrew Muehlig in his peony garden in Ann Arbor. Photo by Eck Stanger, *Ann Arbor News.* Courtesy Ann Arbor District Library.

France, reportedly to have been bought for $250.[3] When he gave up keeping the garden, at least some of the plants were moved to the Peony Garden at Nichols Arboretum.

Like many amateur growers around the country, Weinberg frequently named his peony hybrids for family members and friends. These included a double white named for his wife Elenore and another named for his nephew Bobby Faust. Of particular interest is the variety he named for Andrew Muehlig and introduced in 1928. He entered 'Andrew Muehlig' in the Michigan Peony and Iris Society annual show in Battle Creek in June 1935 and took home first prize for the best seedling,[4] bringing honor both to himself as the originator of the hybrid and to Muehlig, for whom it was named. The peony was described "as of the rose type, with a perfectly-shaped compact rose flower, its guard petals a deep soft rose blending to a cup-shaped center of deep silvery pink. The plant is described as tall and erect and the flowers of exceptional color, form and size, that make it an outstanding variety that is choicest of the fine collection."[5] At some point, 'Andrew Meuhlig' made it into the collection of

Carl Weinberg's award-winning peony hybrid 'Andrew Muehlig' found in the Peony Garden.

peonies at Nichols Arboretum, where it continues to bloom every year. For many years, the name of this variety was misspelled in records at the arboretum, and the unique story behind the variety was lost. While most other of the varieties developed by Weinberg and Muehlig have likely disappeared, this one variety serves as a reminder of the creative breeding done by peony enthusiasts in the early twentieth century.

The Peony Garden at Fair Lane

Karen Marzonie

Fair Lane, the iconic country estate of Clara and Henry Ford in Dearborn, Michigan, was built in 1915 and served as their sanctuary and oasis for over three decades. This National Historic Landmark is significant primarily for its association with Henry Ford and the role he played in American history as inventor, businessman, industrialist, and conservationist. However, the estate's lesser-known significance stems from the role of various designers who gave shape to Fair Lane, particularly the gardens and landscape, which were mostly designed by noted landscape architect Jens Jensen between 1914 and 1921.

At one time, Fair Lane was home to a large peony garden with approximately twelve hundred plants of some forty varieties.[1] The garden was constructed between the fall of 1922 and the spring of 1923 next to an informally spaced apple orchard across the road from the main residence. This would have given the family a lovely view of the garden upon arrival to and departure from their beloved home.

The peony garden was most likely laid out by the head gardener at the time, Mr. Williamson, and installed by his staff of gardeners, including Alfons De Caluwe, who later became the head gardener in 1924. The shape of the one-acre garden resembled a butterfly, as seen in aerial views photographed in the 1930s. A hand-drawn record plan of the estate from 1926, however, suggests that the undulating peony garden shape was not specifically designed to mimic a butterfly. Therefore, it is possible that over time, as peonies were added, the butterfly shape evolved to become more pronounced.

No original planting plans have been discovered to date, but a combination of black-and-white photographs, oral histories, and letters in the Henry Ford and Fair Lane archives provide some clues as to the scale and grandeur of the peony garden. De Caluwe, the head gardener until Clara Ford's death in 1950, stated in his 1952 oral history, "That was the best collection of peonies, at the time, there was."[2] Similarly, a visitor to the gardens from Montreal, Canada, wrote a lovely handwritten letter to Mrs. Ford in 1928, gushing, "Your Peony Garden was the finest I saw again this year and I spent over a week doing nothing else but visiting Peony fields and gardens in the U.S."[3]

A few letters in the archives document that Mrs. Ford and De Caluwe purchased peonies from Farr Nursery Company in Pennsylvania, Iriscrest Nursery in Fort Wayne, Indiana, and Edward Auten Nursery in Princeville, Illinois. Some of the varieties purchased in September 1929 from Edward Auten Jr. included 'Aureolin', 'Mikado', 'Fuyajo', 'Ganoko', 'Isani Cidui', 'Toro Red Japanese', 'Single Red Officinalis', and 'Scarf Dance'.[4] Mrs. Ford even attempted to obtain a permit to import tree peonies from V. Lemoine & Son in Nancy, France, but was turned down by the US Department of Agriculture in 1928 with the explanation that the proposed use did not provide sufficient public value. To the contrary, it is well documented that Mrs. Ford hosted numerous teas and garden walks for local and national garden clubs, women's clubs, and large groups of nurses from Henry Ford Hospital, who likely experienced and enjoyed the seasonal peony display.

The peony garden is thought to have been removed in the 1950s, after Clara Ford's death, but was reconstructed near its original location in 1982 as a much smaller garden (approximately one-tenth the original size). The Garden Club of Dearborn—of which Mrs. Ford was the first president—supported this endeavor with

Preceding page: Fair Lane peony garden. From the collections of The Henry Ford, Dearborn, MI.

Aerial view of Fair Lane. Peony Garden is located to the upper right, across the entrance drive from the mansion. From the collections of The Henry Ford, Dearborn, MI.

The original peony garden at Fair Lane was in the shape of a large butterfly. From the collections of The Henry Ford, Dearborn, MI.

fundraising, planting, and maintenance assistance. A letter in the Fair Lane archives describes the design intent of the scaled-down peony garden. The estate's assistant director in 1982 wrote to the Garden Club of Dearborn, "Using as many of the same type of the original plants as are available, the body of the butterfly would be planted with white plants and the wings with red and pink plants."[5] Approximately one hundred peonies were planted in the reconstructed peony garden that continues to be maintained by Fair Lane gardeners and volunteers.

At the time the Fords built Fair Lane, the site was on the outskirts of what was then the small village of Dearborn, surrounded by farm fields interspersed with woodlands, especially along the floodplain of the Rouge River. After Clara Ford's death in 1950, Ford Motor Company obtained the property and later donated it to the University of Michigan to build its Dearborn campus. Today, Fair Lane is surrounded by two busy arteries of the Detroit Metropolitan area—Michigan Avenue (US 12) and Ford Road (Route 153)—and near Interstate 94 and the Southfield Freeway (M-39). Although just minutes from these major roadways and from the bustling urban core of Dearborn, Fair Lane remains an oasis of open lawns, gardens, and wildlife habitat along the Rouge River.

In 2013, ownership of seventeen acres of the original Fair Lane estate grounds and historic buildings transferred from the University of Michigan–Dearborn to a newly formed nonprofit organization. This organization envisions restoring the entire estate back to the way Henry and Clara Ford originally intended it. The gardens at Fair Lane continue to be lovingly maintained and shared for public enjoyment.

See more at chicagobotanic.org

Chicago Botanic Garden

Nina Koziol

Peonies have long been an important part of the plant collection at the Chicago Botanic Garden, and it's no wonder. Peonies have deep roots in the Midwest.

Century-old peonies still survive in pioneer cemeteries and on abandoned farmsteads across Illinois.

The Chicago Botanic Garden houses more than eighteen hundred peonies growing in fifty-eight locations across its twenty-seven display gardens. In its Midwestern climate, herbaceous peonies bloom between April and June.

Peonies are part of the garden's permanent collection, which holds 2.6 million living plants on 385 acres.

The Garden seeks out plants that thrive in Chicago's challenging soils and fluctuating weather. For peonies, that means traveling to collecting sites across the globe based on their similarity to growing conditions in Chicago.

These collecting trips have yielded breathtaking plants. A 2018 trip went to the remote Vashlovani Reserve in Georgia, a country in the Caucasus region of Eurasia.

There collectors found thousands of flowering fernleaf peonies (*Paeonia tenuifolia*). "Each flower was the size of a salad plate, and a deep, intense red," said Boyce Tankersley, Director of Living Plant Documentation. "The whole population was two and a half to three feet in height, with an equal width."

It can take six to seven years from seed collection and propagation to planting in the display gardens in Chicago. Before any new plants move into the garden's permanent collections, they are evaluated for potential invasiveness.

What's Tankersley's favorite peony at the garden? "I like peonies that don't need to be staked. They're easy to grow and they're unsung heroes that offer a strong structural component in the landscape."

See more at https://www.rbg.ca/

The Royal Botanical Gardens Peony Collection

Alex Henderson

The Spring Garden (now known as the Laking Garden) was the first feature garden developed at Royal Botanical Gardens (RBG), in Ontario, Canada. It was designed by curator Matt Broman in 1945–46 after he secured a large collection of 250 herbaceous peonies from Niagara Parks. The first peony to be accessioned for the Spring Garden was 'Adolphe Rousseau', a double *lactiflora* group with large dark, lustrous red flowers with shades of maroon and yellow stamens. In 1946, 175 plants were acquired from C. F. Wood's family estate Woodeden, near London, Ontario. In 1949 the peony beds were planted in shades of pinks through to reds surrounding the existing iris beds. Japanese cultivars and singles were separated from large doubles depending on plant structure, color sequence, and flower form. In 1954, during bloom season, the Spring Garden was described as being the first truly magnificent display of iris and peonies ever seen in Canada.

During the early 1960s the collection was augmented with tree peonies imported from Holland. As the collection developed, interest in tree peonies flourished, with donations to update the collection.

In 2012 the iris and peony collections were redesigned with improved growing conditions to safeguard the collection for future generations of Canadians. Intersectional hybrid peonies were added. The collection is part of the American Public Gardens Association's Plant Collections Network, which aims to coordinate a continent-wide approach to germplasm preservation among public gardens. Today the collection, while not the largest in North America, is one of the most diverse, displaying a significant number of cultivars that do not occur in other public garden collections.

The Benjamin Harrison Presidential Site's Peony Garden

Bethany Gosewehr

Indianapolis is an economic and cultural crossroads for the Midwest, and in the heart is the Benjamin Harrison Presidential Site. The Italianate structure was President Benjamin Harrison's home from 1875 to 1901 and is where he held his famous "front porch" campaign for the presidency in 1888. The residence annually welcomes nearly thirty thousand visitors from almost every state and over forty countries.

The twenty-third president and his wife, First Lady Caroline Harrison, shared a love of gardening. The museum carries on his legacy with gardens that are beautifully restored and cared for by seasoned volunteer gardeners, many of whom are master gardeners.

The National Historic Landmark grounds feature the Caroline Scott Harrison Herb Garden, Arbutus Garden Club Four Seasons Garden, Centennial Perennial Garden, Freedom Garden, and Presidential Lilac Garden. The gardens provide a visual oasis for visitors and showcase varieties that would have grown when Benjamin Harrison was president.

In 2011, the museum's lead gardeners attended a presentation showcasing hundreds of heritage peonies at the University of Michigan for advanced study and identification. This presented a unique opportunity for the museum to incorporate heritage peonies in the gardens, and the partnership continues to flourish and grow. In the month of May, the abundant blooms and fragrance harken back to Harrison's era and the golden age of Indianapolis.

Visitors love to stroll the grounds while awaiting their museum tour. The Benjamin Harrison Presidential Site is proud to serve as a satellite location for a University of Michigan historic peony project, and further accentuate the legacy of an American president.

See more at https://bhpsite.org/

See more at https://espacepour lavie.ca/en/botanical-garden

The Peony Collection of the Montreal Botanical Garden

Stéphane Bailleul

The Montreal Botanical Garden peony collection is located in the Flowery Brook Garden, where a bubbling brook meanders beneath stately trees and culminates on the shores of a charming pond. The peonies share this idyllic space with the iris and daylily collections, and this grouping gives this garden a distinctive rural feel. In fact, it is not uncommon to see artists set up their easels in the cool shade of this garden.

The peony collection is quite diversified, including both classic and modern representatives of the best peonies in culture. For example, the collection holds bright yellow flowered peonies such as the classic 'Age of Gold' introduced in 1948 by Arthur P. Saunders and more modern varieties such as 'Prairie Charm', an Itoh intersectional hybrid, introduced by Don Hollingsworth in 1992. The tendency in the last decade has been toward acquiring brightly colored single and semi-double flower cultivars of Itoh and herbaceous hybrid peonies. However, Chinese peonies, tree peonies, as well as the dainty fernleaf peonies, among others, are also well represented.

Peonies are also featured in the Japanese and Chinese Gardens, where less sizeable collections are held. Of particular interest was an important shipment of plants, representing some twenty or so Japanese varieties, sent by the Ofuna Botanical Garden for the inauguration of the Japanese Garden in 1988.

In all, some twenty species and close to three hundred cultivars comprise the peony collection. When to name her favorite peony, recently retired horticulturalist Renée Pichette admitted that, among many, her heart went out for Saunders's 'Earlybird', a primary hybrid between two species, *Paeonia tenuifolia* and *P. anomala* subsp. *veithchii*.

The Minnesota Landscape Arboretum Peony Collection

David Stevenson

Development of the Minnesota Landscape Arboretum Peony Collection began in 1961 just four years after the Arboretum's founding. The initial acquisition of nineteen cultivars was obtained from Sylvia Saunders of Clinton, NY. One year later the collection was relocated to a more favorable location, and cultivars were added from local Minnesota nurseries Wedge and Orchid Gardens to bring the number of plants to forty-five.

By 1964 the collection had grown to 143 plants and received support from the Minnesota Peony & Iris Society. Many of the cultivars added during this period were produced by local breeders. The collection features 13 of the 39 cultivars produced by Lins Glad & Peony Farm from nearby Cologne, MN, which began breeding peonies in the 1920s. In the 1960s and 70s, the Arboretum accessioned some 69 peonies from Faribault's Brand Peony Farm, which was operated by O. F. Brand and later his son A. M. Brand from 1867 to 1956 and introduced well over 100 cultivars.

In 1956 the Tischler brothers purchased the Brand nursery, which they ran until the late 1970s before Bob Tischler started Tischler Peony Garden. Tischler operated until 2002, introducing over 40 of his own cultivars, and the Arboretum continued to acquire these plants over the years.

The collection, having grown to 203 plants, moved again in the mid-1970s. It then found its way to its present location in Chaska, MN, in the 1980s. The collection was endowed and dedicated as the Lang Peony Walk in 1990. The collection currently holds 229 accessions of peony. The Peony Collection is one of the premier collections at the Arboretum. The connection to Minnesota nurseries and hybridizers is and will continue to be an important emphasis.

See more at https://www. arboretum.umn.edu/

Whistling Gardens

Sisson's Peony Gardens and Whistling Gardens

Emajean Westphal and Darren Heimbecker

In 1920 Wilbur Sisson planted Sisson's Peony Gardens on a half-acre in Rosendale, Wisconsin. In 1929 he hired Jess Phillips to build a stone windmill in the gardens. Phillips soon took over the garden's care and developed it as a successful business, shipping peonies all over the United States and a few foreign countries. By 1950 the gardens encompassed five acres, and within a few years Phillips had hybridized several varieties, which he named after family members: 'Tinka Phillips', for his daughter, 'Owen F. Hughes', for his grandfather, and 'Kathryn E. Manuel' for his aunt. In 1968, Gov. Warren Knowles honored the gardens and declared the second week of June *Peony Week* in Wisconsin. In 2005 the Rosendale Historical Society resurrected the original half acre and continues to maintain it, adding seven raised beds in 2007. The original windmill still welcomes the public to this cherished garden on the National Register of Historic Places.

Whistling Gardens is a new 22 acre botanical garden located in southwestern Ontario. The gardens feature approximately 1,250 varieties of peonies, including wild species, hybrids, tree peonies, and herbaceous varieties. Recently, most of the tree peonies were moved into the conifer garden for understory color. Bloom typically begins the first week of May and finish by the first week of July. Nearly all of the peonies have been donated by noted Canadian plant specialists and collectors Joe and Hazel Cook and David Maltby, past president of the Canadian Peony Society. Both donors are actively involved in the American Peony Society as well. A formal peony garden was designed and laid out in fall 2016. More information is at www.whistlinggardens.ca

APPRECIATING HISTORIC HERBACEOUS PEONIES AND OTHER HISTORIC GARDEN VARIETIES

other varieties that are very promising but with which we are not yet familiar.

GMR. W. L. GUMM the Veteran peony grower of Remington, Indiana, started with peonies many years ago. He, too, like most people who grow peonies and have a real love for the flower had not been long at the work before he planted seed and through the many years he has been working he has produced several very fine peonies. Lillian Gumm is undoubtedly his best production. This is a great pink. The color is very uniform and distinct and we consider it a very fine flower. Mr. Gumm's Vera, is also very fine. This is a single bright dark red.

MR. L. D. GLASCOCK of Joliet, Illinois, has worked to hybridize officinalis with Chinensis and has a good many promising hybrids.

MR. GEORGE HOLLIS of South Weymouth, Mass., who died in 1911, was one of the early originators of peonies. He named a large number of seedlings but only one of the large number of seedlings stands out in our estimation as really a first class peony, and this is the variety Loveliness. This is a very fine peony and will be found in our general list. This is a large, flat, rose type flower and one of the very late ones to bloom. It is rarely seen at our peony shows for this reason. The color is a uniform hydrangea pink changing to lilac white. It is also fragrant, and when it comes good is one of the very best flowers of the entire season.

MRS. SARAH A. PLEAS of Whittier, California, was a most ardent and diligent worker with her seedling peonies and has the distinction of seeing two of them attain a very high rank. We refer to the variety Jubilee, a wonderful white beauty and Elwood Pleas, a very fine pink. She has the further honor of being the only woman originator of note in the country.

MR. J. F. ROSEFIELD of Indianapolis, Indiana has given us the variety Karl Rosefield, an immense bright red. It is both a splendid cut and show flower. At the American Peony Society's exhibition held at Fort Wayne, Indiana, in 1926, he exhibited two seedlings that gave considerable promise. While he has produced several seedlings, Karl Rosefield at the present time is his one outstanding production. At the time Karl Rosefield was introduced, Mr. Rosefield, the originator, lived at Omaha, Nebraska and this wonderful flower was brought out there. He now lives in Indianapolis, Indiana.

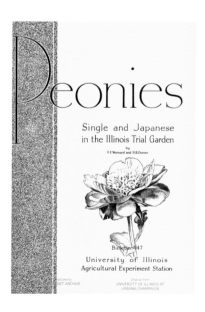

JOHN RICHARDSON of Dorchester, Massachusetts was a peony breeder of very high order. He worked on a limited scale but he loved his work and was painstaking. Walter Faxon and Milton Hill are his two outstanding varieties. He also produced Rubra Superba and Grandiflora. These two peonies are desirable on account of their late blooming habit. Grandiflora makes a wonderful show flower while Rubra Superba gives needed color to a garden late in the season.

Professor Robert T. Jackson of Peterboro, New Hampshire, was a very intimate friend of Mr. Richardson and upon Mr. Richardson's death the peonies were turned over to him. Hovey & Company of Boston, put the varieties, Dorchester, Norfolk, Grandiflora, Rubra Superba, and Milton Hill on the market. The balance of Mr. Richardson's were retained by Mr. Jackson.

To Mr. A. H. Fewkes of Newton Highlands, Mass., must be given the credit of saving for us the variety Walter Faxon or at least bringing it to the attention of the flower loving public. We quote from Mr. Fewkes's letter as follows:

"It was through me that Walter Faxon was brought to notice. Professor Jackson gave me a root of each of the entire collection. In June of the same year that he gave them to me, I went to his place in Cambridge to see them in flower and he called my attention to one he had named Walter Faxon. It was a large plant with a lot of flowers that are shown now on the exhibition tables. I remember his remark at the time that 'the ladies like it,' for the color is nearly a pure pink.

"He sent me the roots in the fall and I think about three years after I exhibited flowers of it at the peony show at Horticultural Hall. They were fine blooms and certainly made a sensation. They were well colored and everybody went wild over them. This was the first time it was ever shown in character and started the demand for it which is still active."

HANS AND JACOB SASS, brothers, living at Benson, Nebraska have worked considerable with peony seedlings and so far have brought out what promises to be a very fine peony, Florence Macbeth.

PROFESSOR A. P. SAUNDERS of Clinton, N. Y., has produced and placed in commerce but three varieties of peonies but all three are very desirable, speaking well for his critical selection. These varieties are Grace Loomis, a splendid white; Silvia, an attractive semi-double, light pink and Matilda Lewis, a very dark red. Prof. Saunders['s] work with new hybrid peonies is attracting wide attention and he will doubtless have something new to offer along this line in the near future.

E. J. SHAYLOR, of Auburndale, Mass., was very active during the latter years of his life in growing seedlings. He has produced a number of exceptional merit among the best of which are Georgiana Shaylor, Mary Woodbury Shaylor, Mrs. Edward Harding, Cornelia Shaylor, Rose Shaylor, Wm. F. Turner, and Le Jour. In all he originated and named about thirty varieties. He died at Auburndale, October 24th, 1926.

Georgiana Shaylor

MR. TERRY was another American originator who named a great many peonies and put them into commerce, but unfortunately they did not possess the merits required by discriminating growers and collectors. His varieties Rachel, and Grover Cleveland are good, and about the only Terry varieties one now sees.

T. C. THURLOW'S SONS of West Newbury, Massachusetts, have originated a number of very fine peonies which we are listing as follows: A. P. Saunders, Betty Blossom, Black Prince, Cherry Hill, Edwin C. Shaw, Helen, James Boyd, James R. Mann, Katharine Havemeyer, Nymphaea, President Wilson, Pride of Essex, Sarah K. Thurlow, Thomas C. Thurlow and Winnikenni. The work of originating peonies with them is a cooperative work and neither of the brothers, Winthrup H. or George C. Thurlow claims the distinction of originating any particular one of the varieties. They have been very successful and have given to the peony world some splendid varieties.

JUDGE LAWRENCE A. VORIES of St. Joseph, Mo., has been very active in producing seedlings and has brought out several of great merit. These are the varieties Frankie Curtis, Nancy Dolman, Henry Vories and Lady Kate. These seedlings are attracting a great deal of attention and will have to be watched as they have a great deal of merit. Mr. Vories has several other seedlings of promise and is to be congratulated upon his work and the enthusiasm he displays in making annual journeys to the annual peony shows staged by the American Peony Society and bringing his originations for exhibit.

MR. WARD WELSH of Springfield, Ohio, had several very fine seedling peonies coming on at the time of his death which occurred in September, 1927. Among these were two very fine light pinks which were shown at the National Show at Peoria. One of these has since been named Mrs. Ward Welsh.

Historic Peonies in Early America

Peggy Cornett

In early colonial American gardens, historians generally agree, the old-fashioned, double-red European "piony," *Paeonia officinalis flora plena*—introduced to Britain before 1548—was a sure presence. Because this ancient, long-lived, and tenacious species was so often associated with monastic herb and medicinal gardens, the common peony was handed from garden to garden as a valuable medicinal aid even among the Puritans. English herbalists such as John Gerard (1545–1612), John Parkinson (1567–1650), and Nicholas Culpeper (1616–54), among others, were well known to European settlers in the New World, and their published works contain chapters on the distinct curative uses and virtues of both male (*P. mascula*) and female (*P. officinalis*) peonies. The name "peony" itself derives from medicinal associations. In his *Herball, or generall historie of plantes* (1597), Gerard reported that "these herbes tooke the name Peionie, or Paeon, of that excellent physition of the same name who first found out and taught the knowledge of this herbe unto posteritie."

The vivid crimson petals of the venerable garden peonies, both single and double, were likewise highly esteemed. Allusions to the peony's ornamental value can be found even in medieval documents, including Master John Bray (died 1381), physician to King Edward III, whose list of "Flower Garden" plants regarded as essential to please the eye contained "Paeony" among a host of commonly cultivated and native flora of the English countryside, including cowslip, daffodil, hollyhock, lavender, lily, periwinkle, red and white roses, and more.

Prior to 1800, however, very few specific references to peonies in American gardens exist. One of the earliest published observations was made not in the Northeast, but rather in a southern state by Irish naturalist and physician John Brickell, who first recorded "peony, male and female," in his self-published book, *The Natural History of*

Peonies at Monticello

North Carolina (1737). (Brickell, it should be noted, was reputably influenced by the writings of early New World naturalist John Lawson's *A New Voyage to Carolina* [1709] and the letters of John Custis of Williamsburg, who corresponded with John Bartram, Mark Catesby, and Peter Collinson). Philadelphia naturalist and plant explorer John Bartram Sr. (1699–1777) was known to have traded the common peony with several Charleston, South Carolina, gardens in the 1760s, and his nursery, on the banks of the Schuylkill River, listed the common peony, *Paeonia officinalis*, and some varieties as "exotic" garden flowers by the mid-eighteenth century.

In 1771, at a time when Monticello stood at the edge of the Piedmont Virginia frontier, Thomas Jefferson was contemplating landscape plans for the "Open Ground on the West," and envisioning "a shrubbery," or a naturalized setting to be planted with "hardy perennial flowers," including "piny" along with a long, ambitious list of both perennial and annual flowers and bulbs. That Jefferson included peonies as part of a designed and managed landscape for his little mountain is significant. Edwin Betts, who edited and published *Thomas Jefferson's Garden Book, 1766–1824* in 1944, identifies Jefferson's peony as *Paeonia albiflora Pallas*, a synonym for *P. lactiflora*, yet it is more likely that Jefferson was referring to some form of *Paeonia officinalis*. Jefferson's source for his "piny" is unknown. Could it have come from his family's garden at nearby Shadwell, Jefferson's childhood home? Did he observe peonies in the town gardens of Williamsburg, where he lived and studied law at the College of William and Mary during the 1760s? These answers remain elusive. Over a decade later, however, Jefferson again includes "peony" in a detailed "Calendar of the bloom of flowers in 1782," which had been planted that spring. Knowing the circumstances during which he kept this calendar over the summer months when his wife Martha's health was precipitously declining after the birth of their sixth child (a daughter, named Lucy Elizabeth, born May 8) makes this record particularly poignant. His observations end following Martha's death on September 6. Lucy Elizabeth died the following year.

Several herbaceous peony varieties appeared in nursery catalogs and garden literature by the turn of the nineteenth century. In *The American Gardener's Calendar,* 1806, Philadelphia nurseryman, seedsman, and author Bernard McMahon categorized peonies under the heading "Hardy Bulbous and Tuberous Rooted Flowering Plants"

Paeonia officinalis	Common Peony
albiflora	White-flowered do.
laciniata	Jagged-leaved do.
hybrida	Mule do.
tenuifolia	Slender leaved do.

McMahon's *Calendar* contains month-by-month gardening instructions, including directions for planting peony roots in April and, in August, taking up, separating, and transplanting "the roots of Paeonias, Flag Irises, and other hardy kinds of fleshy or tuberous-rooted flowers, whose leaves are now decayed." Perhaps not coincidentally, this was the same year Thomas Jefferson received a personal copy of McMahon's *Calendar*, sent by the author in April, and in an unpublished "List of Flowers, 31 May 1806," Jefferson appears to be following McMahon's instructions when he noted "Peony. Take up & transplt. In Aug."

John Bartram's sons, William and John Jr., oversaw the Bartram nursery 1771–1809, and they continued offering the simple "Paeonia

John Bartram

officinalis, peone" in their 1807 catalog. Around this time, tree peonies (*Paeonia suffruticosa* varieties) were arriving from China into England and France, causing a "peonie mania" by 1814. Their arrival in America soon followed. Ann Bartram Carr, granddaughter of the elder John Bartram, and her husband, Colonel Robert Carr, managed the Bartram nursery from 1810 to 1850. Their listing of "*Paeonia arborea* (mutan), *P. rubra*, and *P. papaviracea*" in 1819 is one of the earliest documentations of tree peonies in America. By 1828, Robert Carr issued a "Periodical Catalogue of American Trees, Shrubs, Plants, and Seeds Cultivated and for sale at the Bartram Botanic Garden, Near Philadelphia" containing an entire section on peonies, with twelve species or varieties of herbaceous and woody sorts:

Paeonia officinalis, Crimson official paeony	.25
P. albicans, Double white do.	.25
P. rosea, Rose coloured do.	.25
P. rubra, double red do.	.25
P. carnescans, flesh-coloured do.	1.00
P. albiflora simples, single white do.	1.00
P. whitleji, Chinese double white, with large and splendid-fragrant flowers 3 to 4.00	
P. humei, Chinese double crimson, with splendid flowers	5.00
P. fragrans, Chinese rose-scented, very fragrant	5.00
P. moutan, *Banksii*, Chinese purple, tree-peony, with magnificent fragrant flowers	5.00
P. rosea, Chinese rose coloured do.	5.00
P. papaveracea, Chinese poppy-flowered white with a purple centre	5.00

P. lactiflora 'Whitleyi', double white, was introduced from China in 1808. *P. lactiflora* 'Humei', a double red variety introduced by Roger Anderson in 1810, was first cultivated in the United Kingdom by Sir Abraham Hume at Wormley Bury, in Hertfordshire. *P. fragrans* was introduced in the UK by Sir Joseph Banks, 1805, and considered the earliest sweet-scented double variety grown in England.

The Carrs continued work with tree peony propagation in earnest. In 1835 Boston nurseryman, seed merchant, journalist, and author Charles Mason Hovey (1810–1887) founded and edited the first successful American periodical devoted to horticulture: *The Magazine of Horticulture*. Hovey made several visits to Philadelphia and Bartram's garden during the Carr period and, in March 1837, wrote an essay on the various operations of the gardens, including "the practice of grafting the shoots of the tree paeony upon the tubers of the common sort . . . we were informed that it answers perfectly, and is a safe mode of increasing this magnificent plant." Hovey went on to note that "it will be a long time before the price of good flowering ones will come within the means of the gardening community in general. This we regret: its great splendor and perfect hardiness render it one of the most desirable of hardy shrubs."

At his Flushing, Long Island, nursery William Prince was cultivating woody peonies by the 1820s. Prince's *Short Treatise on Horticulture* (1828) describes three "Moutan Peony" varieties in his garden, including the *Paeonia suffruticosa* 'Banksii': "Chinese Purple Sweet Tree Peony. . . . Several plants in my garden . . . produce from 40 to 50 flowers annually, and they are planted out . . . in the open ground without protection, where they have been growing eleven years." New York "gardener, seedsman and florist" Thomas Bridgeman would question the hardiness of tree peonies in *The Florist Guide, Containing Practical Directions for the Cultivation of Annual, Biennial, and Perennial Flowering Plants* (1835). Bridgeman recognized about twenty species and varieties of herbaceous and woody peonies, including the "many superb species [that] have of late years been brought from China," but he considered many of the tree peony varieties to be half-hardy and suggested they would best survive the winter in a greenhouse.

By 1829, Prince began offering woody and herbaceous peonies through his famous Linnaean Botanic Garden. His catalog of trees and plants claimed: "No class of flowers has recently attracted more attention in Europe than the peonies. . . . anticipating that a similar taste would be evidenced in this country, the proprietor has, by great exertion, obtained every variety possible from Europe and also a number from China." The Prince catalog reached a wide-ranging audience much beyond the northeastern states. In 1836, in the small Louisiana town of St. Francisville, Martha Turnbull, the wife of cotton planter Daniel Turnbull, ordered from the William Prince Nursery twenty-seven different varieties of dahlia and eleven varieties of peonies for her gardens at Rosedown, a plantation in Feliciana Parish.

By mid-century, a craze for newly introduced "Chinese peonies" (*Paeonia lactiflora*) coincided with the expansion of the nursery trade and means of transportation during the Industrial Revolution. These hybrid types offered many desirable qualities—fragrance, hardiness, sturdier growth habit, and a great variety of colors and flower forms. Nursery catalogs across the United States greatly

expanded their selections of peony offerings. By 1858, William Robert Prince, who had inherited the Flushing nursery, was offering thirty varieties of *Paeonia lactiflora*. During this period several American breeders and growers were raising and introducing many new varieties, including H. A. Terry of Crescent, Iowa, and John Richardson of Dorchester, Massachusetts.

Herbaceous peonies are generally happier in northern climates. An 1878 essay on peonies in *James Vick's Monthly Magazine*, out of Rochester, New York, states: "No flowering plants capable of enduring our northern winters are more satisfactory than the Paeonies. Massive without being coarse, fragrant without being pungent, grand without being gaudy, various in form and color, beyond the possibility of being successfully superseded, they stand in the first rank of hardy flowers."

It is notable, therefore, that many nursery establishments in the upper and Deep South also sold herbaceous varieties by the mid-1800s. In Fayetteville, Arkansas, Jacob Smith's 1844–59 catalogs listed "P. Humee [Humei]; P. Whittleyi Major; Violaria Tricolor, Single Paeony; Double White Paeony; Crimson Paeony; Rosecoloured Paeonie." In 1851–52 Thomas Affleck's southern nurseries in Washington, Mississippi, offered "a few of the finest . . . paeonies," and his nursery near Brenham, Texas, in 1860 offered "Paeonias": "several varieties of blush, rose, pure white, and other colors, very double, and some of them quite fragrant."

Colonial Revival and the Grandmother's Garden

No flower can be set in our garden of more distinct antiquity than the Peony.

ALICE MORSE EARLE, *OLD TIME GARDENS: NEWLY SET FORTH* (1901)

By the end of the nineteenth and early twentieth centuries, peonies ranked among the most desirable of garden flowers in America. Hundreds of peony hybridizers and growers across the country, from Massachusetts to Ohio, Illinois, and Iowa were breeding and flooding commercial markets with new hybrids and seedling selections. Determining synonyms became a growing problem. The American Peony Society was established in 1903 with a specific purpose: "to advance public interest in the peony and especially to straighten out peony nomenclature."

At the same time, a near reverential affection for the old-fashioned early red "piny" as an aristocratic flower prevailed in the memories of gardeners and garden writers. In 1901 Alice Morse Earle fondly recalled "in old new England towns fine Peony plants in an old garden are a pretty good indication of the residence of what Dr. [Oliver Wendell] Holmes called New England Brahmins. In Salem and Portsmouth are old 'Pinys' that have a hundred blossoms at a time—a glorious sight."[1]

In the waning years of Victorian-style gardens, both the old-fashioned European sorts and the "modern" varieties were often situated in the middle of lawns so that they could be admired from all angles. Edward Sprague Rand Jr., noted in *Popular Flowers, and how to Cultivate Them* (1873): "Peonies make fine clumps in the grass; they should be disturbed as little as possible, as they grow stronger and flower better year by year."[2] But, as nostalgia for the simpler, grandmother's cottage garden grew, peonies were often grouped in masses in the border. Louise Beebe Wilder, in her book *Colour in My Garden* (1918), recalled her childhood garden in Maryland: "I remember that there were many clumps of these [May-flowering peonies in crimson, pink, and white] massed against the evergreens that formed a windbreak for my mother's Rose garden."[3] The peony's great appeal, then and now, lies beyond the beauty of its magnificent blossoms. Throughout garden literature they are inestimably esteemed for their hardiness and longevity, resistance to bugs, blights, and diseases, and their clean, tidy, classic form. As Joseph Breck pronounced in *The Flower-Garden; or, Breck's Book of Flowers*, peonies are "familiar with every one as a household friend."[4]

Illustration by Will Simmons of peony garden from Louise Beebe Wilder's *My Garden* (1927). p. 85. "A grand burst of pæonies usually celebrates the arrival of June."

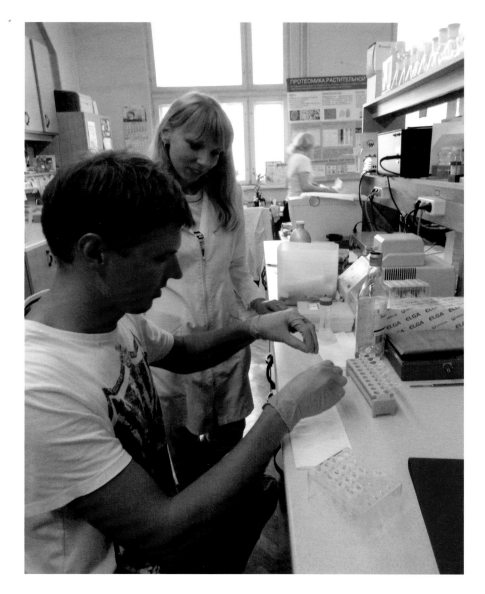

Researchers Andrei Yukhimuk and Elena Agabalaeva studying peony genomic diversity at the Department of Plant Biochemistry and Biotechnology of Central Botanical Garden—Minsk, Belarus. The Garden's peony collection holds more than 350 herbaceous and tree peony cultivars including the best from Soviet, European and American selection programs, as well as endangered *Paeonia* species. More information is at: http://cbg.org.by/index.php/

chloroplast gives the maternal line only. But it has the nuance that any mutation that survives will be passed on to all descendants of the mother's line. Going back to the family passport issue, we now have keys to different kinds of information that together can help correctly configure relationships, and not just group by physical or social similarity, as in the traditional model.

Since 2013 the formal Memorandum between our two institutions recognizes our living Paeonia collections as field laboratories where each peony is a rigorously defined reference specimen. The garden thus becomes ideal for studying peony genome-environment interactions with the potential for powerful predictive models. This includes theories of plant-pathogen genome interactions as well as insights for advanced peony breeding in this era of climate change. To our knowledge, the Peony Garden is unlike any other major display garden (let alone any peony garden), in that there are nearly seven hundred mapped planting spots that have been tracked since the 1920s. What is critically significant is the cultivars are in adjacent pairs—what researchers call "biological replicates." The garden and its nearly 350 pairs of cultivars is the horticultural example of a long-term study site of twins, now going on one hundred years. Thus some aspects of proposed research can be retrospectively evaluated through longitudinal analysis, too. We started to work establishing genomic profiles of cultivars, beginning with four molecular marker systems. With this kind of data we could establish each cultivar's likely parental as well as deep ancestral relationships. With initial partners in Belarus and the Plant Collection Network across North America, and with subsequent expansion once the model was proven, we would have the data to convincingly map the currently unknown "family tree" and domestication history of ornamental peonies. That would be a powerful tool for conservation decisions. Even part of that information would help us with selecting cultivars for conservation in our gardens.

Genomics Helps and Capture Enough of Other Potential Values

Our combined approach of fusing insights from extensive genomic data with both the conventional plant-heritage model and new insights on the social history related to the values sought in peonies during their era of introduction is transforming the beloved Peony Garden and its sister garden at the Central Botanical Gardens in Minsk, Belarus. They are emerging exemplars of reference collections that are as powerful in interdisciplinary research as they are stunning in their public beauty. Now the issues in determining which cultivars to include in reference gardens can move to capturing the spectrum of biological diversity while including a spectrum of all the major aesthetic categories. This approach is also likely to capture the potential medicinal and other nonfloral values of peonies, since the net is wide but uniform.

A shocking first result emerged from fifty cultivars judged diverse based on criteria from the traditional model. We had trialed a particular molecular method with a Soviet-bred cultivar whose immediate parentage with wild-collected species is well documented. The molecular method confirms it. For our fifty

Facing page: Zhemchuznaya rossyp. Photo by Valentina Gaishun and Natalya Lunina.

cultivars, we were surprised the genomic-based evidence caused the relationship clusters to be "inverted". The species branched off far to the left (as expected), with the ancestral species (*P. lactiflora*) being a "sister" to all the cultivars that are understood to have been bred within that species (also expected). The problem was the subgroups. The French set among the fifty cultivars is *the most distant from the ancestral species, but it is historically the oldest for the European cultivars.* This is why we love science. Either the data have errors, or the interpretation has errors, or possibly both. The expectation in studies as this is the older cultivars will cluster with the ancestral species, on the assumption that they were bred first. After much discussion and rechecking, we realized that the assumption that the French cultivars were the oldest was a fallacy. Of course they were based on Chinese cultivars introduced into Europe in the early 1800s (see Peggy Cornett's "Historic Peonies in Early America" in this volume). One can see that the Soviet-era cultivars cluster as a group. That's not a surprise when one considers the breeding stock came from France, mostly after World War II, and that new ornamentals were likely being bred by using wild species native to the Soviet Union. So the Soviet cluster's location closer to the other species makes sense. The missing key is Chinese cultivars, a small selection of which are only recently growing at the Peony Garden as honored gifts from the Luyoyang Tree and Flower Garden. As they say, watch this space as we work with our plants.

An entirely new angle emerged from the genomic work: several virus genomes were found and are being published in GeneBank.[1] Some of these viruses appear to be "silent"—that is, the peonies don't show obvious symptoms of being infected. It is possible some viruses may be beneficial. Regardless of which viruses are present, for conservation it is necessary to remove any that are pathogenic and reestablish virus-free plants. This is common in many fruit crops, as seen in advertising of virus-free strawberries and raspberries to home gardeners. The standard approach is to tissue-culture the plant that has the virus, treat the tissue culture, and regrow virus-free plants from there. But herbaceous peonies never read the book and are considered intractable for tissue culture. It rarely works. Again, we love science! Is the problem that the process doesn't work with peonies, or that peony physiology has something to teach us—that we're being too simplistic? This is an active area of research with our colleagues at the Central Botanical Gardens in Minsk, with funding from the Belarusian Foundation of Fundamental Research and the University of Michigan's peony initiative.

Valentina Gaishun (in blue), curator of the National Peony Collection of the Central Botanical Gardens, National Academy of Science Belarus with peony conservation colleagues Veronika Filipenya, Hanna Viarouchyk and Nastassia Vlasava. The Central Botanical Gardens and the Nichols Arboretum each have extensive peony holdings not represented by the other, giving them together a conservation research tool with many exceptionally rare and significant living specimens.

Putting the Eggs in More Than One Basket: A Network of Peony Gardens

The Peony Garden at the Nichols Arboretum is a founding member of a peony group in the Plant Collection Network. These gardens span North America from Alaska to Quebec and south to Nebraska and Pennsylvania. The current set of gardens holds just over fourteen hundred peony cultivars, but most cultivars are at only one garden: literally one step from horticultural extinction. For the consortium to thrive, each public peony garden has to have its own mission-driven focus, which complicates assembling as comprehensive a collection as possible. However, this also means that there are many areas of specialization, in our case, the peonies favored by Dr. Upjohn, as well as others for a representative collection introduced before 1950.

Ultimately in our network of research gardens, beginning here and at the Central Botanical Gardens in Minsk, we seek to maximize capturing all aspects of peony diversity for enjoyment and research of generations ahead. Embracing more gardens that share this approach expands the scope of conserved cultivars and increases redundancy. It's important to have redundancy—that is, having specimens of the same cultivar at different gardens. Should there be a calamity at one site (a natural disaster or a new pest), then the other sites can be the sources for the future. A robust network keeps the eggs in more than one basket.

Genomic Tools Will Unmask Dr. Upjohn's Missing Peonies

Across North America there are likely thousands upon thousands of beautiful peonies without a name. These are persisting and thriving in parks, cemeteries, old homesteads, perhaps even your garden, where they may be a treasured family pass-along from a beloved relative. Even major gardens such as the Peony Garden and the Central Botanical Gardens have their "unknown" accessions. These peonies are too beautiful, treasured, and vigorous to remove. But what were their original names? As we and other research gardens enlarge the pool of verified peonies with "molecular passports," these unknowns can be addressed one by one. When the molecular passport matches, we know the plants are clones—and thus restore the name. Nearly matched unknowns should cluster with their close relatives. From there the historical literature should provide the names of likely candidates for the next iteration of "Could this be its original name?" For some, we'll never know, but we'll know their closest relatives. These will likely be the ones that were introduced without a name, or, as in the case of some of Auten's cultivars (see "Edward Auten Jr.: Peonies That Are Different" in this volume), sold as one of a kind. In addition are the untold number of peonies that may have been cross-pollinations by busy bees and the home gardener or cemetery keeper never noticed that a new and slightly different generation had established.

The Peony Garden at the Nichols Arboretum has at its core a living "snapshot" of what Dr. Upjohn thought epitomized beauty in peonies, augmented with selections from peers. It is our goal to find the missing ones that were once growing here based on our historic inventory maps. Perhaps viruses overtook them, at least for display quality? Or did a staff member not like them and so remove them? We'll never know, but so far we have found no other gardens or specialist nurseries that grow them. But as we develop our genomic tools and skills—including viral cleansing—there is both hope and expectation that many, if not all, can be found. Returning them for a complete, historic, living documentary of his vision will be a significant accomplishment, even if it extends beyond our lifetimes.

We return to where we began, but with a deeper appreciation and new ways to think as we quest to conserve the best of beauty. Now it is clear that beauty alone will deceive us when assembling a comprehensive conservation collection of ornamental plants. To endure the challenges of the future, our collection must be robust as well as meritorious. For that, the genomic framework, including emerging issues in landscape-scale genomic interactions with other organisms and pathogens in the environment, is critical to safeguarding the beauty that is here. We like to think Dr. Upjohn, at heart a researcher who reveled in the beauty of peonies, would rejoice.

Color Is More Than Pigment

Floral color is more than just a pigment. Petals are many cell layers deep, and each layer of cells as well as different parts of the flower (such as veins) may have different concentrations of the same—or closely related—pigments. In addition, the microscopic roughness of the outermost cell's surface affects the scattering of light, resulting in exquisite nuance to the color's depth. Yellow to orange colors are based on an entirely different chemical system of pigments than the one that underpins pinks, reds, and some blues. It surprises most visitors to know that white is not a pigment in plants. It is the opposite—the absence of any pigment. The white is from the cell walls scattering the sunlight so that all of the visible spectrum is reflected. That is the definition of "white" light. Thus for a peony flower to fade white means the pigments are degraded. To open white or blush (a light pink) and get deeper-toned means the pigment is being increased or activated. The peony genus (but not any given peony) captures the entire color spectrum except (so far) pure blue. Floral pigments are a wondrous world of their own.

Visitors to the Peony Garden are also surprised to learn that the floral colors are not assessed under direct sunlight and for consistency, "color" is the hue of the top (apical) flower the day it opens. It's important to note that peony flower colors may change subtly to dramatically from bud opening to end of bloom, often displaying complex shades and sheens that are difficult to describe— this is part of their appeal! Historically, color terms were not standardized and are best taken as a descriptive range rather than an absolute unless listed as "pure" or an equivalent term. Color terms often reflected a particular writer's flower repertoire or commercial objective—thus "red" may have been their reddest seen to date, rather than an abstract color value.

Yablochkina. Photo by Valentina Gaishun and Natalya Lunina.

Vecherniaya Moskva. Photo by Valentina Gaishun and Natalya Lunina.

Fragrant Peonies

Harvey Buchite

Peonies offer one of the best examples of the sweetness of smell that we refer to as fragrance. Besides the appearance of large, striking blooms in many colors and forms, it is their intoxicating fragrance that individuals remember and want to establish in their own gardens and fresh bouquets. While time may have exaggerated the perfume in our memories, it is true that many peonies do not have the strength of fragrance possessed by the older *lactiflora* varieties of grandma's garden.

Fragrance can be characterized by its relative strength and its type. In the garden a strongly scented peony allows you to enjoy the fragrance at a normal viewing distance, while some peonies require you to get right up close to enjoy what may be a heavenly, but more moderate in strength, fragrance. These moderately fragrant varieties are sometimes appropriately used indoors, without a worry about the fragrance being overpowering. The more strongly fragrant varieties can be used in moderation in the vase to good effect when combined with less fragrant but lovely varieties. Fragrance changes during the day and depends on temperature, humidity, and the age of the flower. Blossoms just being warmed by the early morning sun upon first opening are often at their peak of fragrance and later, in the heat of the day, may not be significantly fragrant, as the volatile essential oils are evaporated from the flower.

Having grown many hundreds of varieties of peonies, I can tell you that *all* peonies are fragrant. Some peonies have the fragrance of roses or a pleasant citrus spice—while others smell like a fish that has been sitting in the bottom of a boat in the sun! Some people find the sharp fragrance emitted by the pollen of single and semi-double flower forms pleasing, while others wrinkle up their nose in disgust. The scent is sometimes described as medicinal. However, as the pollen dries on the single flower forms, the sharp fragrance generally

becomes less noticeable. To dismiss all the single flower form peonies, then, would be a great mistake. For display in the garden, their fragrance is not detrimental unless you have your nose right in the bloom. And some do indeed have a pleasing smell.

The following not only are some of the most fragrant but also superb for cutting and bringing indoors: 'Duchesse de Nemours', which holds its sweet fragrance throughout the life of the flower; 'Baroness Schroeder', noted for its rose fragrance; and 'Kelway's Glorious', which has a marvelous rose fragrance almost identical to 'Mme. De Verneville'. 'Mme. Emile Lemoine' has a pleasant, sweet fragrance with a crisp citrus undertone. 'Philomele', a wonderful French variety from the Victorian Era, is a tricolor peony having a mock orange fragrance, but not as strongly scented as the mock orange shrub. The true 'Festiva Maxima' has a distinct rose fragrance too, although not as fragrant as some of the previously mentioned varieties. Unfortunately, it is difficult to find the true variety, as many low-budget discounters pass off any white double with a splash of red in the center, of which there are many, as 'Festiva Maxima'. The real thing grown next to impostors is easily identified as a truly wonderful variety. Another variety noted for a fragrance similar to roses is the enormous double white 'Ann Cousins', which is a very impressive, well-formed double with good healthy foliage all season. Its size does require that it be given some support in the garden, but it is well worth the fifteen seconds needed to place a support hoop each spring as the plants emerge. 'Mandaleen', a double pink variety with a rose-like scent, was introduced by Lins and is avidly sought out by peony collectors.

Anyone who cares to take the time to sniff a great number of peonies will find that the list of those with pleasant scents grows longer in the color range of white, blush, and pink varieties, well ahead of the red varieties, which more often have stronger, not quite pleasant, undertones. Among the pinks we have 'Mons. Jules Elie', 'Alexander Fleming', 'Doris Cooper', 'Mister Ed', 'Miss Eckhardt', 'Princess Margaret', 'Myrtle Gentry', 'August Dessert', 'Bess Bockstoce', and 'Chestine Gowdy', all having excellent fragrance. When one does find a red double with good fragrance, it is worth noting and adding to your collection for the variety of bloom color, and for a longer period of color, since many bloom just ahead of the double pinks and whites.

Fragrant double white and pink varieties derived from *Paeonia lactiflora* that bloom toward the end of the season are readily available, and many of these are very fragrant. A few of my favorites include 'Festiva Maxima', 'Louise Lossing', 'Moonstone', 'Mrs. Frank Beach', 'Myra Macrae', 'Myrtle Gentry', 'Nancy Nora', 'Phoebe Cary', and 'White Frost'. These can be smelled from a distance of several feet in a garden and would be overpowering as a large bouquet in a small room. 'Burma Ruby', 'Diana Parks', 'Flame', 'Henry Bockstoce', 'Mary Brand', and 'Postilion' are red and red-tone peonies that are quite fragrant.

Moderately fragrant peonies are those whose fragrance will be evident in the garden in the absence of a significant breeze and delightful in a large bouquet. These might include 'Elsa Sass', 'Fairy's Petticoat', 'June Rose', 'Karl Rosenfield', 'Princess Margaret', 'Raspberry Sundae', 'Red Charm', 'The Fleece', and 'Top Hat'. There are more moderately fragrant than very fragrant peonies and a greater range of color and form in these varieties.

Many other peonies are lightly or slightly fragrant, inviting you to get close to the bloom to really enjoy the sweet scent. There seems to be an endless list of these, including 'Dainty', 'Dandy Dan', 'Felix Supreme', 'Friendship', 'Gardenia', 'Henry Sass', 'Joyce', 'Legion of Honor', 'Longfellow', 'Marie Jacquin', 'Pride of Blasdell', 'Red Grace', 'Red Red Rose', and 'Roselette'.

As with all senses, each person perceives fragrance differently. Our sense of smell diminishes as we mature. Fragrance of a particular variety may also vary with temperature, humidity, time of day, and even growing conditions, although these differences are generally fairly subtle. A very fragrant peony will have significant fragrance throughout the endurance of the bloom. Some hybrid peonies have scents that are generally considered unpleasant.

Moonstone

Postilion

With careful selection it is possible to have fragrant peonies in your garden for several weeks of bloom. As mentioned earlier, the very fragrant *lactiflora* varieties tend to bloom late in the season. It is more challenging to find fragrance among early blooming peonies, but some are at least slightly fragrant, including *P. tenuifolia* 'Hardy Giant', 'Laddie', and 'Early Scout'. Extend the fragrant bloom period by including tree peonies such as 'Golden Era', 'Leda', 'Black Panther', 'Chinese Dragon', and 'Marchioness', as well as intersectional peonies such as 'Unique', 'Bartzella', 'Garden Treasure', 'Hillary', 'Prairie Charm', 'Callie's Memory', 'Julia Rose', and 'Watermelon Wine'. These not only add fragrance but a wider range of flower color, foliage, and plant form. Many of the Award of Landscape Merit peonies are fragrant, in addition to providing excellent landscape plants, including 'Coral Sunset', 'Burma Ruby', and 'Early Scout'.

Whether for garden plants or cut flowers, fragrance is an important factor to consider in selecting a peony. Fragrance will be dispersed by a breeze, so a sheltered location is best if you wish to benefit from the full effect of a fragrant peony. One intensely fragrant plant in the garden or bloom in a bouquet will perfume an area and give the impression of overall fragrance.

Since fragrance is so personal, gardeners are encouraged to visit public gardens, private growers, commercial plantings, and peony flower shows such as the American Peony Society conventions in order to evaluate fragrance for themselves. There is nothing like the real thing when selecting peonies for such an important characteristic.

Fairfield

The Art of Peony Hybridization

Don Hollingsworth

Successful peony breeders are simultaneously botanists, artists, and salespeople. In addition to knowledge about cultivation and hybridization, the best breeders have a creative eye for the incredible palette of peony variation and a sharp sense of how to wield it to satisfy particular needs in the market. I've spent my career honing these skills. In the early years of my work, much of my effort was studying how peonies grow in general, including dormancy, resistance of early buds to freeze damage, and variation in growth habit between different species ancestries. Later, while operating my retail nursery, I concentrated on transferring doubleness into the first three flowering periods—very early to early midseason. More recently, after visiting the late-season cut-flower enterprise in Alaska, I experimented with approaches to breeding white flower cultivars that do not go blush/light pink in cool environments and double-flower cultivars that open satisfactorily from buds (as for show table competitions, where the flower must be cut before the petals fully unfurl and complete opening overnight).

As much as possible, my breeding program focuses on deliberate crosses. I select parents with a particular purpose in mind, not just willy-nilly. Accidental achievements do happen, whether because of opportunity—what is flowering when I have the desired pollen in hand—or the ever-present challenge of contamination by "stray" pollen. Still, my choices about matings are almost always driven by specific breeding goals, which have shifted for me over the years. When I started, I focused primarily on flower character and interspecies fertility. Additional experience led me to prioritize characteristics needed for commercialization and end-user benefits. Perhaps the biggest landmark in the evolution of my "eye" as a peony breeder happened when I became involved in retail offering around 1992. I realized then that, if a cultivar is going to outlive its creator, it must succeed in commerce on its own merits. This idea came into further focus as I crafted item descriptions for our

Don Hollingsworth at Yew Dell Garden with Garden Treasure in foreground and below

catalog. I needed to view my plants from the perspective of end users—not only the cultivar's advantages, but also any significant faults, such as need for support if flowered in a viewed landscape or subject to late freeze damage, as in erratic spring warm-up climates.

Overall, I am drawn to the ornamental qualities and harmony of plant and flower as a whole (landscape end-user viewpoint), vigor and overall performance in relation to conditions provided by the growing environment, and characteristics supporting cut-flower potential—these assets in light of whether the subject plant offers potential for introduction to commerce. My favorite registered cultivar of my own creation is 'Garden Treasure' because of its overall range of ornamental attributes and its top-flight performance. Its vigor is superior, among the most resistant of fungi among the garden peonies, and it is widely adapted in regional climates when typical peony-growing needs are met. Unlike any other peony cultivar known to me, it opens flowers over an extended period, two and a half weeks or more in my regional climate, where spring heat pushes peony flowering, up to four weeks or more at more northerly sites, such as Minnesota and northward. It is highly suited for landscape applications, and fields of it are producing for the florist trade in the both the Northern and Southern Hemispheres, said to be the only Itoh hybrid suitable for the purpose. Semi-double to double flowers are well formed, golden yellow; deep green, attractive foliage compares well, lasting through the summer, with the better lactiflora cultivars in this respect.

On a more personal note, 'Garden Treasure' resulted from a cross I made in my second season of breeding peonies, 1968. The story: by 1967 or so I knew the history of the four Louis Smirnow introductions of the yellow-flower hybrid plants bred by Toichi Itoh of Japan (a lactiflora cultivar × pollen of Lutea hybrid 'Alice Harding'). A year or so later I determined to repeat the cross, but I did not have the pollen in sight. I wrote to the garden editor of the *Kansas City Star*, who also did landscape design services, expecting he might be a better-than-average source of where peony 'Alice Harding' might be found in KC gardens. He did not know, but when his weekly newspaper column appeared the following Sunday, the subject of his column was my story and appeal. I did not expect much from it, but to my delight a few days later there surfaced a fellow in Independence, a suburb on the eastern fringes of the metro area, pleased as punch to know he had something rare. I had my pollen, but meanwhile my peonies were all bloomed out. A few days later was the Memorial Day holiday and our annual trip to Maryville to visit my wife's parents, right where I live now. Along the driveway were very old peonies, one of which had a few side-bud flowers remaining, to which I applied my pollen. That autumn I collected five seeds, three of which were germinated indoors over winter and in time made leafy shoots. When planted outside to grow, within days some worm-size beast managed to cut through the root on one of them, resulting in its loss. Of the two remaining, the best became 'Garden Treasure'. It made excellent growth the first year, was moved the first autumn, made the second season of growth, and flowered the following spring. Within a few years it became evident we not only had achieved one of the first American bred Itoh hybrids, but one that is especially healthy and having an unprecedented length of flower opening period, two and a half to four weeks or more, depending on how hot the spring warm-up.

My Love

I try to evaluate new cultivars a relatively long time before putting them on the market. Having an abundance of space to hold seedlings while increasing them is a contributing factor. Introduction depends on having increased a candidate to a desired quantity. My practice has been to not register a name until we decide to introduce it in the upcoming annual catalog. When seedlings first flower or within a season or two, some will be selected for further observation. We have normally divided and grown to maturity for at least two cycles before any decision to cull. Reselected items are then grown in propagation cycles, pending a decision to name and introduce.

Peony breeding is a great creative outlet and offers pretty much a level playing field, very little big-operator competition. The investor money goes to species that afford a quicker turnover. We compete with hobbyists and sometimes small retail growers. Getting started need not require a bunch of cost. For most of us, we at first did some crosses of opportunity, just to see what happens. No detailed study necessary beforehand. However, when the first ventures turn into enthusiasm, study becomes a valuable tool. Look at the titles offered at the website www.AmericanPeonySociety.com. Also have a look at the Yahoo groups of peony breeders and join the American Peony Society for current information on new cultivars being registered by breeders who have been at it for a while.

The Enduring Value of Historic Peonies

By Scott Kunst

What Makes Historic Peonies Special?

But why bother with old peonies, you might ask. Aren't the new ones better? Breeders today *are* developing peonies in a wider range of colors and forms than ever before, and many of these new varieties are vigorous and sturdy. But older peonies are definitely worth saving—and growing in your own garden. Here are a few reasons why.

Older peonies are great garden plants.

They're gorgeous, as the thousands of visitors wandering blissfully through the Peony Garden every June will tell you.

They're wonderfully diverse—short, tall, early, late, with blooms that come in six different forms and a myriad of colors from deepest maroon through endless shades of rose and pink to purest white.

They're often fragrant, and richly so. In fact, on lists of the most fragrant peonies, older ones typically outnumber newer varieties by a wide margin.

And they're time-tested, having proven themselves over many years and in a wide variety of growing conditions to be tough, adaptable, and enduring—and isn't that what we all want in our garden plants?

Older peonies are priceless genetic storehouses.

Although it's hard to predict the future, it's sure to be different. The

climate will probably be warmer. New pests, diseases, and weeds will challenge us. And our collective vision of beauty, nature, and what a garden can be will continue to change. To meet the needs and wants of this unforeseeable future we need to preserve the incredible genetic diversity that's stockpiled in older peonies and other heirloom plants.

The dangers of a lack of genetic diversity were made all too clear in the Irish potato famine of the 1840s. When a deadly blight attacked what was virtually the only potato variety being grown in Ireland then, over a million people died and another million had to flee the country in order to survive.

Of course no one will starve if we don't save historic peonies, but preserving the genetic diversity of garden flowers makes sense, too. Back in the 1960s, for example, hybrid teas were the only kind of roses most people grew. Although they were beautiful, most varieties were highly susceptible to fungal diseases, which meant they had to be sprayed with poisons on a regular basis. Eventually most gardeners decided that wasn't a great idea, but what roses could they grow instead?

Luckily some outside-the-mainstream gardeners were still growing older, unfashionable kinds of roses that didn't require fungicides to stay healthy. In time breeders used these all-but-forgotten older roses to breed new types for the twenty-first century including David Austin's English roses and low-maintenance "landscape roses" such as the Knock Out series. Flourishing without poisons, these popular new varieties would never have been possible if the genetic diversity of older roses had been lost.

Older peonies are time machines.

Not literally, of course, but if you appreciate antique quilts, Victorian houses, Mission-style furniture, or 1950s Chevrolets, you probably understand what I'm talking about. Just like other historic relics, older peonies offer us tantalizing glimpses of a world that's disappeared and—even better—a chance to look at our own world with new eyes.

"The past is a foreign country," wrote novelist L. P. Hartley, "they do things differently there," and whether you're traveling the globe or going back in time those different ways of doing things can open your mind to unexpected possibilities. Whether you discover a delicious new food in Quebec or a cool new esthetic in *Mad Men*, your tastes are broadened and your life enriched.

For gardeners, the past offers countless visions of beauty, nature, gardens, and whatever it is that makes some flowers so special that

Preceding page: 'Studies of Peonies' by Martin Schongauer, circa 1472. Courtesy J. Paul Getty Museum.

PASSION FOR PEONIES

we want to grow them ourselves. We can explore these possibilities, and choose the ones we like best, but only if we can see, smell, and grow the plants that gardeners back then loved—which is exactly what the Peony Garden offers us.

Historic plants also offer us a living connection with loved ones and kindred spirits who gardened before us, deepening our feelings of rootedness and belonging. Whether it's a marigold Thomas Jefferson grew or your grandmother's favorite peony, when it blooms in your own garden I think you'll find the feeling is something special.

Extinction in the Garden

But if older peonies are so great, why are they disappearing?

Throughout history, as the needs and wants of gardeners have changed, so have the plants we've chosen to grow in our gardens.

Take hyacinths, for example. For much of the eighteenth and nineteenth centuries, hyacinths were *the* most popular spring-flowering bulb, with one Dutch nursery in 1874 offering some 1,700 varieties.

But then the world changed. Daily bathing and deodorants gradually became the norm, making richly fragrant flowers such as hyacinths less captivating. The rise of central heating made forcing them into winter bloom more difficult, since they require temperatures under 48° F to root well, and advances in transportation technology made heat-loving subtropical houseplants an affordable substitute. Then as the Victorian enthusiasm for carpet-bedding waned and a more naturalistic planting style came into vogue, the formal, orderly look of hyacinths—which had been part of their appeal for centuries—fell increasingly out of fashion.

As a result, most bulb catalogs today offer fewer than a dozen hyacinths, and almost all of the 1,700 varieties grown in 1874 are now extinct. When a plant is in high demand, as hyacinths were back then, or hostas and daylilies are today, nurseries can profitably offer a vast range of varieties. But when demand ebbs, that profusion doesn't make sense economically and—no matter how wonderful they might be—many varieties are lost forever.

Will hyacinths ever be wildly popular in the garden again? Only time will tell, but many other plants have rebounded after falling out of favor. Ornamental grasses, for example, were a stylish choice in late Victorian gardens but largely forgotten for most of the twentieth

Ferry Hyacinth

century. Then in the 1970s a few savvy gardeners rediscovered their virtues and before long they were on their way to becoming one of the signature plants of our gardens today.

Peonies have had their ups and downs, too. For their first two hundred years in American gardens, they were a decidedly minor plant, with only a few varieties of the European *Paeonia officinalis*—valued since ancient times for its herbal properties—commonly grown.

That changed dramatically, though, with the introduction of *Paeonia lactiflora* from China in the early 1800s. Long celebrated in Asian gardens and art, peonies there had been diversified into hundreds of varieties, and the first to arrive in the West caused a sensation. Not only were they new, beautiful, and sweetly fragrant (unlike *P. officinalis* whose scent is at best "spicy"), they also came from an alluringly exotic land.

By the 1850s, French breeders had introduced scores of new varieties, including enduring favorites such as 'Edulis Superba' (1824) and 'Festiva Maxima' (1851), which are still widely grown today. British and American breeders soon followed suit, and peonies remained a popular garden plant for most of the century.

America's enthusiasm for peonies peaked in the early twentieth century. The American Peony Society was founded in 1903; American breeders such as Brand of Minnesota introduced scores of the era's best new varieties; and wealthy gardeners embraced them. Clara Ford, for example, the garden-loving wife of Henry Ford, filled her one-acre, butterfly-shaped peony garden with some 1,200 plants, and W. E. Upjohn launched the University of Michigan Peony Garden by donating plants from his private collection of more than 600 different cultivars.

Peonies were also one of the era's most popular cut-flowers, in part because they could be picked in bud, transported without water in refrigerated boxcars, and then, days or even weeks later, coaxed into bloom as easily as if they were freshly picked. You can try this at home—without the boxcars—and enjoy peonies in bloom months after you pick them.

With the coming of the Depression, though, peonies went into a long decline. They were no longer "must have" plants and played only a limited role in gardens of the 1950s and later, which emphasized evergreen foundation plantings, hybrid tea roses, groundcovers, and annuals.

The effects of this slumping demand can be seen in the peonies offered by the Sherman Nursery of Charles City, Iowa. Founded in 1884, by 1925 the nursery was growing millions of trees, shrubs, vines, and perennials—including 130,000 peonies.

When I stumbled upon it in the 1970s, Sherman's was wholesale only but it still offered an impressively long list of peonies, many of which dated back to the nineteenth century and could be found nowhere else. Even as late as 2001 they were offering 111 different varieties. But then floods and the Great Recession took their toll, and in 2009 the nursery was sold to a much larger wholesale grower— which today offers just two dozen peonies. Although this no doubt makes sense economically, those of us who love the rich diversity of peonies will find it hard to see it as anything other than a loss.

Preserving Historic Plants around the Globe and at Home

The Peony Garden's work is part of a growing plant conservation movement, which in turn is part of the broader environmental and historic preservation movements.

Although so far most "Save the Plants" efforts have focused on wild species and food crops, ornamental plants are increasingly recognized as worthy of preservation, too. In fact, in its 2011 Global Strategy for Plant Conservation the United Nations cited the need for protecting not only the genetic diversity of food crops but also—for the first time—other "culturally valuable species" such as ornamentals.

Botanical gardens in the United States have slowly begun to expand their traditional focus on collecting and protecting wild plants to include garden cultivars as well. In 1996, for example, the American Public Gardens Association established the Plant Collections Network, which now includes more than 130 Nationally Accredited Plant Collections. Although most of these are devoted to wild varieties of trees and shrubs, a handful are conserving garden perennials such as hostas (Toledo Botanical Garden), clematis (Rogerson Clematis Garden), and the treasures of the Peony Garden.

The world leader in the conservation of garden plants is the British nonprofit Plant Heritage. Founded in 1978 as the National Council for the Conservation of Plants and Gardens, Plant Heritage has grown to encompass some 640 National Plant Collections, most of which are dedicated to garden plants such as daffodils, hardy geraniums, and lilacs. Some of the collections are quite broad while others are more narrowly focused such as dark-leaved dahlias, iris bred by Sir Cedric Morris, and "Queen Mary II Exoticks."

Unlike the Plant Collections Network that is limited to public gardens, in the United Kingdom anyone can apply for National Collection status, and as a result most collections are in private hands. Nearly half belong to individual gardeners, another third are held by commercial nurseries, and the rest are cared for by city parks departments, universities, historic sites, and botanical gardens.

Plant Heritage and the collection holders are supported by almost forty regional chapters that help with research, garden care, and outreach. There's also a Threatened Plants Program to identify varieties most in need of protection, a Plant Guardians program that encourages members to grow at-risk plants at home, and a popular annual Plant Exchange.

Here in the United States, a few organizations such as the Cultural Landscape Foundation and the Southern Garden History Society

Benton Menace iris, bred by Sir Cedric Morris

are dedicated to historic gardens and landscapes. Others such as the National Trust for Historic Preservation include gardens as part of their broader missions. Unfortunately, none are doing much to save historic garden plants.

Luckily a handful of other groups are. In the American Rose Society, older roses are championed by the Old Garden Roses and Shrubs Committee and most ARS shows offer awards for historic roses. There are also two national organizations devoted to older roses—the Heritage Rose Foundation and the Heritage Roses Group—as well as several local groups such as the Texas Rose Rustlers and Heritage Roses Northwest.

Another important organization is the Historic Iris Preservation Society, a section of the American Iris Society. Founded in 1988, HIPS offers a wide array of activities and services. At its website, for example, you can view photos and descriptions of well over 2,000 iris, read scores of articles dating as far back as the 1890s, and even get help identifying that nameless iris from your own grandmother's garden.

Like most plant societies, the American Daffodil Society was once focused solely on the latest new varieties. That began to change, though, in 1997 when I lead a small group of fellow enthusiasts who convinced the ADS to add a section for "Historic, Pre-1940 Daffodils" to all daffodil shows across the country. Since then the section has become so popular with both ADS exhibitors and the general public that a section was added for "Classic Daffodils" dating from 1940 to 1969. The society also has an active Historic Daffodils Committee that works to "encourage gardeners, public gardens, and ADS exhibitors to grow historic daffodils in order to assure their preservation for the pleasure and use of future generations."

Hopefully the efforts of these groups will inspire other plant societies to develop a more inclusive view of what's blue-ribbon worthy and their missions overall. As exciting as the latest varieties may be, they're only one small piece of any plant's story and appeal, and celebrating the diverse beauty of every era can help plant societies draw new members and thrive.

Thousands of historic sites and museums across the country include ornamental plants in their gardens and grounds, and most include at least a few historic varieties. Those few that plant only carefully researched historic varieties and explain to visitors how they're different and why they're important certainly deserve our applause. Unfortunately it's rare for a museum site to consider historic plants as part of their preservation mission—just like the buildings and other artifacts that are in their care—and I for one hope we see more of that in the future. It's not only botanical gardens that ought to be conserving historic flowers.

Commercial sources also have an important role to play. Hundreds of heirloom vegetables, for example, which were once all but impossible to find are offered today by scores of mail-order catalogs. The same isn't true for heirloom flowers, though, and many sources offer mostly modern varieties of flowers with a long history in gardens rather than truly historic ones. Take snapdragons, for example. Although *Antirrhinum majus* has been grown in gardens for centuries, not all snapdragon varieties are heirlooms—a distinction that's clear to most people when it comes to, say, tomatoes, but much less so when it comes to flowers.

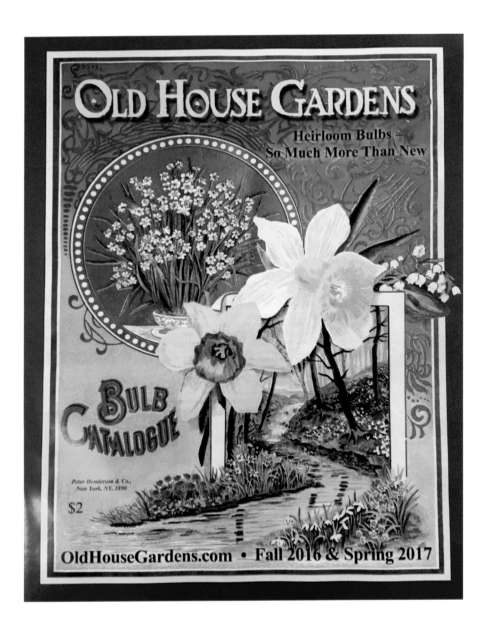

Luckily a few small specialist nurseries here in the United States do include some truly historic flowers in their catalogs. Among those with unusually rich offerings are the Antique Rose Emporium, Heritage Flower Farm, Superstition Iris, Adelman Peony Garden, Hidden Springs Flower Farm (peonies), Bloomingfields Farm (daylilies), Select Seeds, and my own small mail-order company, Old House Gardens.

I launched Old House Gardens in 1993 when my favorite tulip was dropped by the one last catalog that offered it. Richly fragrant and returning better than any tulip I'd ever grown, the 137-year-old 'Prince of Austria' was just too good to let go extinct.

I mailed my first tiny catalog to 500 people, and when complete strangers sent me money and encouragement in return, I thought, "This might actually work." Twenty-four years later I retired and sold my business to one of my employees, and although too many incredible old flowers slipped through our fingers over the years, I'm proud to say that Old House Gardens is still going strong—and you can still find 'Prince of Austria' in its catalog.

Prince of Austria tulip

What Can You Do to Help Save Historic Flowers?

Support the Peony Garden. Visit, bring your friends, share its beauty online, join the Friends of MBGNA, donate, volunteer (see peony. mbgna.umich.edu/get-involved), and repeat!

Join plant-preservation groups like HIPS and others mentioned above.

Advocate for historic plants in the plant and garden groups you belong to and at the historic sites and public gardens where you work or volunteer.

Grow and enjoy historic flowers—including family heirlooms—in your own garden.

And pass these amazing flowers along, so future gardeners can enjoy them, too.

PEONIES IN CLASSIC
GARDEN WRITING

From The Book of the Peony

Alice Harding

Alice Harding (Mrs. Edward Harding) (d. 1938) was a well-respected gardener in the early twentieth century, especially known for her expertise on peonies, lilacs, and irises, three of her favorite flowers. Born in New Hampshire, she and her husband, Edward Harding, a prominent New York lawyer, chose to live in Plainfield, New Jersey, where they created extensive gardens and she collected and experimented with many garden flower varieties. Known for her garden writing, she wrote the classic *Book of the Peony* (1917), from which these selections are reprinted, and *Peonies in the Little Garden* (1923), particularly helpful for new gardeners. One of the most revered peony varieties, 'Mrs. Edward Harding', was named in her honor in 1918 by E. J. Shaylor, who won the $100 prize Mrs. Harding offered for the best new peony introduction that year. She offered a similar prize for the best new French peony seedling in 1922. The prize was won by the well-known breeder Emile Lemoine, who named the variety 'Alice Harding'. In addition, a tree peony, two irises, two lilacs, and a rose were named in her honor.

In this discussion, she describes her deep appreciation for peonies and provides background on their history.

An Appreciation of the Peony

Full of set flowers,
Full is my chamber;
Thou art most stately,
White peony.

—HAKKU.

THE BOOK OF THE PEONY

BY

MRS. EDWARD HARDING

WITH 20 ILLUSTRATIONS IN FULL COLOUR
22 IN DOUBLETONE AND A MAP

PHILADELPHIA AND LONDON
J. B. LIPPINCOTT COMPANY
1917

The peony of today—too little known and too seldom sung—the brilliant result of years of steadfast devotion and untiring effort on the part of peony lovers and hybridizers, is the most superb and commanding flower which the garden holds. The iris, Oriental poppy, fox-glove, holly hock, lily, dahlia and chrysanthemum each has its own special radiance, yet each is surpassed by the peony with its magnificence of mass and perfection of detail. The rose, fine, exquisite and fragrant as it is, must yield first rank to the modern peony, which by reason of its sheer wealth of splendour and majesty of presence is now entitled to be called the Queen of Flowers.

The compelling charm of the improved types of peony lies not only in their grace and comeliness, but in the infinite variety of both flowers and foliage. Starting with single blooms, like huge anemones, through semi-double flowers, resembling water-lilies, and various enchanting forms of doubling up to the solid mass of petals, as in Avalanche, the peony holds one spell-bound in admiration. The wide diversity of foliage and habit of growth makes the plants an object of alluring interest. The leaves of certain sorts of peony are much divided and fern-like; of others, broad and strong with leathery quality. Usually varnished and lustrous, they run in colour range through many shades of green—often tinged with copper or with red. Some kinds are dwarf and bushy; some of medium height and spreading growth, and others tall with a bold outline. All, however, have an air of sturdy character and self-reliance.

Fondly as I esteem the rose—heretofore the accepted standard of loveliness—I feel that the peony has the advantage over it, not only in superiority of flowers, but in other important points. The peony has no thorns to surprise or cause dismay. After the peony blooms its foliage remains an adornment—a contrast to the small and scanty leaves of the rose, which are often disfigured and unsightly. All through the garden season the peony has a landscape value which the rose lacks. And, last but not least, the peony requires neither spraying nor pruning: to the conscientious owner, burdened with the numberless details of spring garden-keeping, this is a welcome relief. . . .

For those who as yet know the peony only in a general way, I will set out in orderly array no less than seven distinct and excellent reasons for considering the peony the best of all perennials:

1. **The sightly appearance of its blooms**. The elegance of the flower, its different forms, the satiny texture of the petals and the numerous tints and shades of white, pink and red make its

fairness a never-ending joy. In many kinds there is also found fragrance equal to that of the rose.

2. **Its worth for both landscape and cutting.** Both in mass and in detail, it answers many requirements. The substantial size of the plant and of the individual flowers makes it a useful and striking subject for the garden architect. The brightness, sweetness and lasting qualities of the blooms make it an ideal cut flower.

3. **The freshness of its foliage throughout the summer.** A number of perennials lose the freshness of their foliage after blooming and have to be cut back or hidden by other plants. Except in one or two instances, the shining foliage of the peony attracts attention from the time of its appearance above ground until it succumbs to the late frosts.

4. **The ease of its culture.** Anyone can raise peonies successfully with far less trouble than it takes to grow roses.

5. **Its practical freedom from insects and disease.** While a number of diseases of the peony have been classified and described, the grower who reads and heeds directions is not likely to be troubled with diseased plants.

6. **Its extreme hardiness.** It thrives in very severe climates, and endures a degree of cold that is fatal to many other perennials.

7. **Its permanence.** Lifting and dividing the roots are not necessary for at least eight or ten years. Many varieties can be left undisturbed for fifteen years or more.

The Mythology, and Ancient and Modern History of the Peony

The peony has been such a familiar flower in humble gardens in this country that many persons are not aware of its aristocratic and extended genealogy. The descent of the peony can he traced through numerous periods of history even into mythology; indeed in Greece, the Roman Empire, China, Japan, France, England and America, its relation to mankind has been considerable.

In medicine, art, commerce and science, the peony has played a part which not only entitles it to general recognition, but which is also absorbing in detail. At different times in the past, it has been the object of many journeys and voyages, the subject of years of painstaking study, and to its improvement men have lovingly devoted a large portion of their lives. From Leto, mother of Apollo, who appears to have been the original "introducer" of the peony, down to M. Dessert, the great French grower, who in 1915 sent out his latest peony under the name of "Victoire de la Marne," we have a long and entertaining story, of both horticultural and human interest. . . .

The Peony in Mythology and in the Classics

Zeus and Leto were the parents of Apollo, god of healing, who was the father of Æsculapius, god of medicine. According to the ancient writers, Paeon, pupil of Æsculapius and physician of the gods, first received the peony on Mt. Olympus from the hands of Leto. With it he cured Pluto of a wound inflicted by Hercules during the Trojan war. To quote from Homer's Iliad with its stirring action: "Pluto also endured a swift shaft when the same hero (Hercules) the son of Ægis-bearing Jove, afflicted him with pains at Pylos amongst the dead. But he went to the palace of Jove on lofty Olympus, grieving in his heart and transfixed with pain; for the shaft had pierced into his huge shoulder and tortured his soul. But Paeon healed him, applying pain-assuaging remedies."[1]

This cure caused so much envy in the breast of Æsculapius that he secretly plotted the death of Paeon: probably the first recorded instance of professional jealousy. But the wicked plotter was destined to be foiled. Pluto, in gratitude for what Paeon had done, saved the physician from the fate of mortals by changing him into the plant that had been used in the cure. This plant has ever since borne Paeon's name.[2]

The history of the cognate word paean is interesting as showing some of the possibilities of etymology. After the time of Homer, the name of healer and the office of healing were transferred from Paeon to Apollo, who was thenceforth invoked by the cry "Io Paean" sometimes made to him as physician and at other times made to him irrespective of his healing art. Subsequently, a paean was a choral song to Apollo or Artemis, his twin-sister (the burden being "Io Paean"), in thanksgiving for deliverance from evil. Later it was addressed to other gods on similar occasions,[3] and then to mortals. Now it is a "loud and joyous song": witness this book.

The peony was known to Greek writers under the name paeonia and also under the name glucuside—"having sugar qualities"—evidently referring to the honey secretion of the flower buds. It is mentioned in the works of a number of early authors, among whom are Pliny, Theophrastus, Dioscorides and Galen.

Pliny, in his Natural History (about 77 A.D.) gives the first detailed description of a peony plant and seeds, but does not mention the flower. He says: "The plant known as paeonia is the most ancient of them all. It still retains the name of him who was the

The truly wild *Paeonia lactiflora* (formerly *P. albiflora*) from northern China and the Russian Far East is seldom seen in gardens. Flowers with a single row of petals approach the wild-type elegance.

first to discover it, being known also as the 'pentorobus' (from its five seeds which resemble vetches), by some and the 'glucuside' by others. . . . It grows in umbrageous mountain localities and puts forth a stem amid the leaves, some four fingers in height, at the summit of which are four or five heads resembling Greek nuts in appearance; enclosed in which there is a considerable quantity of seed of a red or black colour. This plant is a preservative against delusions practised by the Fauni in sleep (nightmare). . . ."[4]

Pliny devotes one chapter to a fuller description of the plant and sets out twenty ills or diseases of the human body which it will cure. Among these are jaundice, gnawing pains in the stomach and certain affections of the trachea. He says it acts as an astringent and then adds: "It is eaten also by beasts of burden, but when wanted for remedial purposes four drachmae are sufficient."[5]

Dioscorides, a medical man who flourished in the first century of the Christian Era, describes about five hundred plants in his Materia Medica. The peony is included in this work. The famous Viennese Manuscript of Dioscorides, painted and written in Byzantium for the Princess Anicia Juliana in the early part of the Sixth Century, contains a number of brush drawings of plants and flowers, some of which closely resemble our specimens of to-day. Unfortunately, the illustrations of the two peonies mentioned in the text—Paeonia arren [*P. corallina*] and Paeonia theleia [*P. officinalis*] are missing. The lifelike representation of his favourite flower was evidently too great a temptation for some peony lover to resist.

Herbaceous Peony History in China and Japan

In China and Japan the popularity of the herbaceous peony was somewhat overshadowed by that of the tree peony, but the former kind has long had a distinct recognition in both countries. In China it was called "Sho Yo" meaning "most beautiful," which bespoke a considerable appreciation on its own account, even though the tree peony was ranked as the King of Flowers. It served as a sort of Forget-me-not which one friend bestowed upon another on separation. A Sho Yo plant was also presented for a friendly remembrance after separation. These customs are referred to in a Chinese song:

If anyone will give his friend a present
He hands a gift "most beautiful" of all.

In 586 A.D., the herbaceous peony was fairly well distributed over the country and was used for medicinal purposes and in a number of places even for food for human beings. The appreciation of its dietary value was another instance of the advanced character of the civilization of China, for the peony as a source of nourishment was surely but the prototype of some of our modem breakfast foods. Hung King writing at this time, distinguished two sorts, the red and the white, which is the first mention we find anywhere of a white peony.

In 968, Mas Ze, an author on natural history and natural philosophy, discoursed learnedly at considerable length on the herbaceous peony. In the early part of the Eleventh Century, according to another Chinese historian of the period. the herbaceous peony was grown in all parts of China but the most valuable roots came from the district of Huni Gan Foo—wherever that was. By 1086, as a literary botanist of that date tells us, gardeners realized the possibilities of the plant for ornamental purposes and began, by the application of strong fertilizers and great diligence in cultivation, to produce flowers of large size. As a result of these efforts and the extensive propagation by planting of seeds, new and better varieties were produced. In 1596, more than thirty improved kinds were listed in the catalogues of Chinese growers.

Among the number of beautiful things for which Japan is indebted to China, few equal the peony. Early in the Eighth Century, the Japanese imported from China both the herbaceous and the tree peony. The herbaceous peony was called "Skakuyaku"—apparently a corruption of the Chinese Sho Yo—and has been highly thought of, although not accorded the honours given the tree peony, which is ranked as one of the three Royal Flowers.

In Japanese literature and folklore the peony is the subject of many poems and stories. It is not clear in each case from the translation whether the herbaceous or the tree peony is referred to, but it is evident that both kinds were cherished in the hearts of this flower-loving people. There is a little Japanese verse that shows that East and West meet in the kindred pleasures of the garden if nowhere else:

When Spring is on the wane,
*   Then men are apt*
To turn their thoughts
*   To peonies again.*

The Fascination of Peonies

Intimate Portraits of the Aristocrats of This Family by One Who Knows Them Well and Loves Them

Louisa Yeomans King

Louisa Yeomans King (Mrs. Francis King, 1863–1948) was among the most important garden writers of the early twentieth century. She was influential in forming two of the most important garden clubs—the Garden Club of America (1913) and the Woman's National Farm & Garden Association (1914), for which she served as the first president. Writing for some of the most prominent garden magazines of the early twentieth century—*Garden Design*, *House and Garden*, and *House Beautiful*—King provided helpful advice on garden composition and layout, plants, color, and horticulture for the small gardens being created for the growing number of homeowners around North America. Her books, such as *The Well-Considered Garden* (1915), *The Little Garden* (1921), and *The Beginner's Garden* (1924), provided additional advice for the home gardener and drew upon her experience in creating her own garden in Alma, Michigan.

In this article, originally published in *House and Garden Magazine* in October 1926, King raves about some of the choice varieties found in her garden.

Long ago I learned that really to see Peonies they should be so grown that one could sit near or actually beside them. So I sit now on this twenty-eighth day of June, the fragrance of countless Mockorange blossoms filling every air that blows, and the most glorious flowers

Francis and Louisa King in their garden. All photos used by permission of Clarke Historical Library, Central Michigan University.

that we have for our gardens, bar none, close at hand on their respective plants.

'Jubilee' is before me in full sun, its milkwhite feathers of petals moving in the breeze, its beautiful pale lemon-colored central cup very distinct in the bright light. 'Midsummer's Night's Dream' is beside my straw chair (all these Peonies are set in round holes in grass) and I can lift one of its luscious heavy heads and see its creamy center flaked with carmine and admire its guard petals of pale lilac and the general look of its handsome flower. At a little distance is 'Reine Hortense', with its warm pink hue in the young flower and its fine tuft of white petaloids or true carpels. In the near distance stand two plants whose flowers glow like rubies. 'Felix Crousse', not new, but so fine and 'Ville de Nancy', beautiful in form as in color, the clearest most vivid of carmines, without any traces of purple, or of violet, a dazzlingly bright carmine.

And now I move my chair a few yards on among older, larger plants, and sitting beside these my eyes seem to be opened for the first time to the charm of Peony Alsace Lorraine, whose scalloped white beauty with its central flush of pale yellow, is so enchanting. This Peony, says Mrs. Harding, should not be disbudded. Certainly the effect of countless symmetrical flowers on one great plant is uncommonly fine. Here too is Marie Jacquin with its Waterlily form and roundness, its great size, and with us unfortunately, its rather weak stem. However, for such troubles, we have now the remedy. The *Bulletin of the American Peony Society* for June, 1926 has this item in the Secretary's notes: "*a sample of ——'s Peony supports has been received. These will be found a splendid support, one of the best I*

have ever seen." Mrs. Christman is an authority on such matters. No sooner had I seen this, our early Peonies at the moment in fat bud, than I rushed to the typewriter and sent for a few. I agree with the Secretary that better supports for Peonies were never offered.

Three feet high now are three beautiful plants of C. S. Minot, the interest of whose form, the exquisite light pink of whose flower is beyond this pen to describe. In some ways this Peony suggests Thérése. Hard by is one precious specimen of Mrs. C. S. Minot, a flower which seems modeled in wax with creamy white reflections towards the center and tiny flakes of pure carmine near the stamen. What a flower this is and what a rare straight stem here too—a stem which possibly realizes that it carries a Caesar among peonies!

Such charming flowers as Marie Lemoine, Mme. Emile Lemoine, La Rosiere, Rosette, with its pretty rounded pink flowers, Raoul Dessert, a wonderful pink from Chenonceaux, Marie Crouse with its shell pink bud and chiseled blooms, cameo-like as they open, Claire Dubois's astounding globes of cool pink petals, Kelway glorious with feathery cream like flowers of great size and most interesting form, Vcnus's delicate beauty, delicate though in a large flower—these in large measure make up the range of what we call the "block." Here are some of our special treasures. Many of these were presents from no less of a personage in the world of Peonies than Mrs. Edward Harding herself. And to her suggestion is due this square of open cultivated ground where these fine plants have a better chance for life than those set in the turf, even though a foot in all directions is kept open around the latter. Today these Peonies in the block are such a feast for the eye that it is hard to compose the mind for even the slight physical and mental effort of writing. Slight however the mental effort need be when such subjects for the pen present themselves. The feelings translate themselves into words, the felt words transmute themselves into written ones in an effortless fashion. An hour goes by like five minutes, and five or six scribbled pages seem to have written themselves.

In the "block" are such beauties as Souvenir de Louis Bigot, center of so much attention at the Peony Show at Fort Wayne this year, with its rich color and form, its rose and silver beauty. Here too is what is probably the true Edulis Superba (the Cornell Peony Bulletins declare that this variety has eleven synonyms in name!) with its four-foot stems, and fine pink bomb-type flowers. Near it are two pearls of Peonies, Walter Faxon with its unmatchable warm pink, and Solange whose tea-rose hue, whose marvelous camellia-like blooms, must be seen [to fully appreciate and] can hardly be touched upon in writing.

Other Peonies of older sorts there are below shrubs in other parts of these two acres, lovely varieties such as Festiva Maxima, Jeanne d'Arc, Marguerite Gerard, M. Jules Elie, this last still rating high among them all—Mme. de Verneville, Octavie Demay, the heavenly Sarah Bernhardt, and my favorite in late delicate pinks, the charming Mme. Emile Galle. Baroness Shroeder shines forth white and perfect among late Peonies. Primavere is here, with its rare yellow center, clear against white guard-petals; it stands by Marie Crousse, the two forming the perfect pair in Peonies. For delicate color contrast, and this either for planting or for cutting there is no finer association in flowers than this.

Odette gives a beautiful effect on the plant and when cut its broad pale lilac guards are in delightful contrast to the creamy yellow petaloids. A large flattened ball of these form the center of this exceedingly refined flower. Suzette is one of the vivid pinks, a loosely built flower with deep pink guard petals, rising to a high cup-like center. Asa Gray is delicious in semi-shade on a day of heat; and here Lemoine's Lamartine raises its huge balls of deep cool pink, tipped with silver; and Calot's Peony of the same name holds up its soft loosely petalled heads of round pale pink flowers. This Peony has as soft a look as Therese of C. S. Minot, a fluffiness of large petal which is truly arresting. Calot's Lamartine is of a much paler pink than

Lemoine's. Its petals also form a ball-shaped flower but the silvery hue is very marked here on the tip of each petal, in fact is one of the characteristics of the noble flower.

Is there a finer Peony in existence than Richardson's Grandiflora? For color, its pale cool pink, "for form," its rose type, for size—one bloom here this year measures nine inches across, and twenty six in circumference—but here is Martha Bullock another large flower, "center deep rose pink, outer petals shell pink." According to Mrs. Harding, it is impossible to choose between such beauties as these— all call for superlatives.

At this moment a huge humble-bee is clinging to the center of one of the blooms of Alsace Lorraine. How good he is in scale on such a flower, and what an interest he adds to the Peony as part of a composition! He reminds one of the beautiful drawings in color of flowers with their attendant bees by Katherine Cameron in her distinguished book of poems and pictures "Flowers I Love."

The very names of Peonies bring one into the company of gifted, distinguished or heroic people. No one can sit among these flowers as I do now, writing these names, gazing at their beauteous namesakes, without thoughts of France, of England, of those of our own land whose interest in the world of gardening has caused their names to flower upon my ground, to mean so much to me. When such delightful reflections are joined to the tranquility of a fine June day, to an almost absolute seclusion with these marvels of flowers, when to the sweet fragrances of the Peonies themselves is added the intoxicating—yes, no less—scent of the walls of Mock-orange in full flower nearby, this world is little less than Paradise!

This peony-themed kite was produced by the renowned Chinese Kite Master Ha Yiqi as part of a workshop on kite-making and a kite festival held in Nichols Arboretum in September 2011 as part of the fiftieth anniversary celebration of the Lieberthal-Rogell Center for Chinese Studies at University of Michigan.

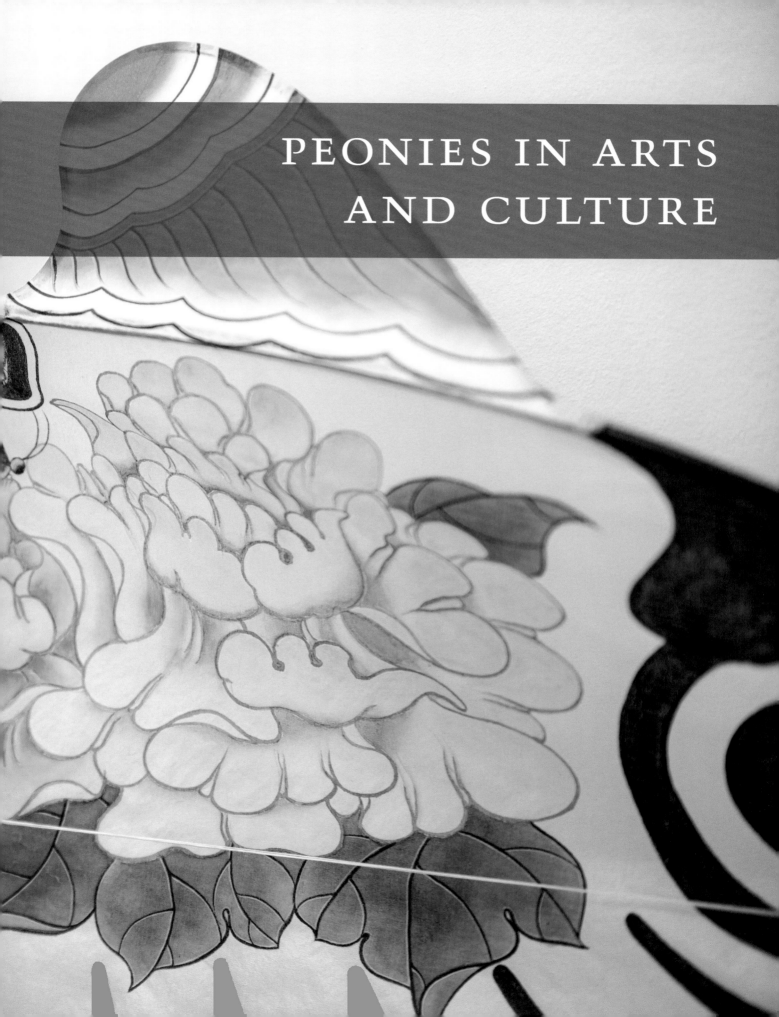

PEONIES IN ARTS
AND CULTURE

The Peony in Painting and Verse in China from the Eighth to the Thirteenth Centuries

Roslyn L. Hammers

The magnificent Song-dynasty (960–1279) painting *Calico Cat under Peonies* (*Fu gui hua li* 富貴花狸) presently in the collection of the National Palace Museum, Taipei, captures the release of peony's beauty as it blossoms through time (*facing page*). At the apex, the tree peony plant (*Paeoniaceae*, sect. *moutan* or in Chinese *mudan* 牡丹) is topped by a densely packed bud, a flower that has not begun to unfurl. Passing over one opened flower, the petals of the blossom below at the center of painting are partially open. As we move to the bloom at the viewer's right, this peony has outer petals that have lowered, revealing the central petals, which are expanding outward. The remaining three wholly visible flowers are in varying stages of blossoming, from just fully opened (at the lower left), to fully opened (located directly below the bud), and then to the flattening of the bloom as the petals dip downward, preparing to eventually drop away. The painting is a technically accomplished feat depicting the cycle of the tree peony's life, a demonstration of the astounding observational skills of the anonymous artist.

Scholars typically discuss the painting in connection with its symbolism. By the second half of the eleventh or the first half of the twelfth century, the date of this painting, the peony was associated with social status and wealth, an invitation for viewers to enjoy auspicious tidings for prosperity.[1] Given its large size (141 × 107.5 cm) it may have been a screen painting, but presently is mounted as a hanging scroll. With its high quality of production, the painting was mostly likely commissioned by the court, and therefore the peony was considered appropriate for costly, large-scale representation.

For modern viewers the appeal of the painting lies in its beautiful representation of the flower and the feline, but if we explore the history of the peony in China, we may further our understanding of the bloom within its historical environment. In this essay, I offer an overview of the peony and its reception in poetry and painting, to interpret and evaluate some of the associations that representations of peonies evoked in early Chinese history.

Early Visions of the Peony: Poetry and Painting

The cultivation of the peony and its cult was inaugurated in the Tang dynasty (618–906), extending well into the present. Shu Yuanyu 舒元輿 (791–835), an ambitious official who lived during the Tang, reportedly composed the first poem written on the peony. His preamble to the rhapsody suggests that in the classical era, peonies were not recorded as they grew in the mountains. Empress Wu Zetian (624–705), who had lived in a remote region, requested that peonies be transplanted to the imperial gardens in her capital city of Luoyang, introducing them to the court and elites. Shu Yuanyu intimates that the empress started a craze. Every spring visitors arrived in Luoyang and went crazy over "one of the greatest spectacles in the country."[2]

In his poem Shu Yuanyu himself may be seen as partaking of the euphoria, effusively praising the beauty of the peony:

我案花品	I note the flower's [the peony's] ranking.
此花第一	This flower ranks the first.
脫落群類	It is outstanding among its kind,
獨占春日	Monopolizing the spring sun
其大盈尺	With a size more than one foot
其香滿室	And fragrance that fills up a room,
葉如翠羽	With leaves like jade feathers
擁抱比櫛	that embrace one another closely.
蕊如金屑	Its pistils are like gold flakes
妝飾淑質	that decorate its fine beauty.
玫瑰羞死	Roses die in shame.
芍藥自失	Herbaceous peonies exile themselves.
夭桃斂迹	Luxuriant peach blossoms become recluses.
穠李慚出	Resplendent plum blossoms leave with embarrassment.
躑躅宵潰	Rhododendron blossoms wilt and flee at night.
木蘭潛逸	Magnolia blossoms steal away.
朱槿灰心	Rosy hibiscuses are disheartened.

紫薇屈膝	*Crape myrtles kneel down.*
皆讓其先	*All relinquish [their positions] so the peony may lead.*
敢懷憤嫉	*There is no reason to be jealous,*
煥乎美乎	*(For the peony is) so lustrous! So beautiful!*

In this verse Shu Yuanyu is quite enthusiastic. For him, the peony, as judged in the court of flowers, is likened to high officials of the first or highest rank. He assigns the peony the role of leader, intimating that the peony and its exalted beauty serve as a metaphor for the emperor. In Shu's verse,[3] the peony with leaves of jade and golden pistils is identified with social status and wealth, associations that continue to this day in East Asian culture. In addition, Shu aligns the peony with men—first-rank officials and the emperor—a combination that is rather surprising, as the peony later becomes associated with seductively gorgeous women, a point to which we will return.

The poem's background may help us understand two representations of peonies in a tenth-century tomb for Wang Chuzhi 王處直 (862–922) and his wife (*right*). Wang was a warlord who lived at the end of the Tang and hailed from an elite military family that produced generals for the imperial Tang army.[4] The murals in the tomb feature the peony in more than one location. One painting depicts a peony bush accompanied by birds and butterflies, seeming to grow out from a perforated rock, a recognizable type of valuable stone harvested from Lake Tai. The painting is done in light colors with relaxed but confident brushstrokes. This rock with its peony and fauna is clearly out-of-doors, and it may simply be represented in the tomb to further establish the presence of a garden setting for the deceased occupants to enjoy. As modern scholars have demonstrated, this type of rock was (and to this day still is) associated with men of unusual character or scholarly personality, and its pairing with a peony further suggests that peonies were not solely identified with beautiful women.[5]

In addition we find peonies were also placed to the side of a landscape painting on the northern wall, and this room of the tomb appears to have been constructed like an artist's studio with views. The inclusion of a monochromatic landscape along with the peony in the tomb underscores the occupant's claims to culture. Scholars have convincingly argued that Tang tombs are meant to reconstruct an ideal life, with luxury items and markers of status as is befitting for the tomb's occupants. Tombs reflect the occupants' temporal wealth and social standing, along with what were thought to be his or her needs for the afterlife.[6] Consequently, in their tomb Wang

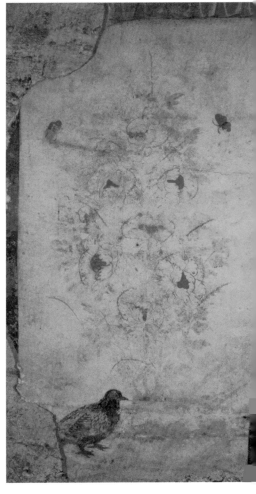

Peonies in the tomb of Wang Chuzhi

Chuzhi and his wife were provided with peonies to appreciate throughout eternity.

During the Tang, the peony also acquired a number of feminine associations for which it is well known. Initially connected to the Empress Wu Zetian, as already mentioned, the flower was identified with another larger-than-life woman, Yang Guifei (719–756), an infamous consort of Emperor Xuanzong (r. 713–756). During the eighth century, in other contexts, the peony's feminine gender roles were consolidated, and the reputation of peony as a sultry, voluptuous, intoxicating beauty reached its apotheosis. This alliance is due to a suite of extraordinary poems by the great Tang poet Li Bai 李白 (701–762) that equate the beautiful consort with the flower.

Yang Guifei was fond of visiting the imperial peony garden, and according to a contemporary writer, Li Jun 李濬 (active 713–727), Emperor Xuanzong and Yang Guifei were admiring peony flowers in full bloom at night in the Sandalwood Pavilion.[7] When the emperor was displeased with the musical entertainment for the celebration, he summoned Li Bai to create other songs. Li Bai composed a suite of three poems collectively entitled "Qingping Melody in Three Parts" that equated Yang Guifei's beauty with that of the peony. The poem suite is justifiably famous, and as it establishes the reputation of the peony, we turn to the first verse. It reads,

雲想衣裳花想容	*Clouds recall her robes, blossoms her face,*
春風拂檻露華濃	*Spring winds caress the rail, dew-laden petals grow lush.*
若非群玉山頭見	*If you do not see her atop Jade Mountain,*
會向瑤台月下逢	*Then surely you shall meet her beneath the moon at Jasper Terrace.*[8]

Jade Mountain and Jasper Palace are names of the abode of the immortal, the Queen Mother of the West. Peonies, the immortal goddess, and Yang Guifei meld into one entity, visualized as frothily enrobed blossoms of tremulous petals. The beautiful woman and beautiful flower swirl provocatively and evasively. That which is being viewed is not fixed, shifting between peony and woman. Like clouds and blossoms, gently buoyed by spring winds and laden with misty dew, Yang Guifei and the peony are transformed into an ethereal presence, floating within a unearthly realm.

The painting *Court Ladies Wearing Flowered Headdresses* depicts women who help us envision beautiful Tang women with flowers (*top of facing page*). In this painting that is probably a version of a Tang original, the flowers that adorn the ladies cannot be recognized

as peonies, but the gorgeous bloom still makes its appearance,
featured on the fan that the maid carries. While none of the
women may be identified as Yang Guifei, the beauties, like
the imperial consort, spend time in a garden setting among
blossoms. While history records that Xuanzong's beloved met
with a tragedy,[9] the peony suffered no such misfortune and
only rose to great heights of spectacular adulation.

Peony Pageants and Their Cultivation

In Luoyang of the eighth and ninth centuries, Tang gardeners
attained great showmanship in their manipulations the peony,
producing hybrids or cultigens in which the flowers' stamens
were transformed into petals to create an exuberantly whorled,
yet compact, corolla. This process is referred to as *qian ye* (千葉)
or "thousand petals" (lit. "leaves"), and the Chinese term for the
flowers created through this procedure can be translated as "double"
blossoms. The obsession with the peony was expressed through
nearly annual celebrations of the creations of all manner of hybrids.

   We know from another great poet, Bai Juyi 白居易 (772–846),
that exquisite blossoms fetched huge sums of money during the
ninth century. His poem "Mai hua" 買花 (Buying flowers) provides
a description of festivities that accompanied the "peony blooming
season" (*mudan shi* 牡丹時).[10] When the flowers begin to bloom,
everyone runs around to purchase them. He notes that the price is
based on their appearance and that an old farmer, having seen the
frenzy at the peony market, sighed, claiming,

一叢深色花　　　*One cluster of deeply colored blossoms,*
十戶中人賦　　　*Would pay the taxes of ten ordinary households.*

If we consider the expense the flowers demanded, we can understand how the peony came to be associated with wealth.

An album leaf painting of a peony, presently in the Hong Kong Museum of Art, carries a problematic attribution to the painter Xu Xi 徐熙 (d. before 975) (*below*). It may very well be a Ming dynasty painting of the sixteenth century or so, but it depicts a Tang botanical possibility, a stunning representation of a twinned, double-bloomed peony. The painting allows us to understand at a formal level the basis for Bai Juyi's critical amazement at the feats gardeners achieved. The peony is skillfully depicted with a sense of three-dimensionality, as light and color play across the surfaces of the petals and the leaves, beautifully rendered with subtle changes in colors. The contours of the leaves curl at the edges, allowing the artist to show viewers their underside. Focusing on the twinned blossom itself, the artist took extra care to call viewers' attention to the extraordinary nature of the flower by inserting at least three leaves into its center. This painting revels in detailed observation of the phenomenal bloom, recording its grandeur for posterity and certainly for the pride of the gardener who engineered it and owner who possessed it.

Courtesy Hong Kong Museum of Art

The Peony: Later Considerations beyond Beauty

As Bai Juyi's sentiments indicate, the accomplishments of the gardeners were not always greeted with glowing appreciation. By the eleventh century, the scholar-official Ouyang Xiu 歐陽脩 (1007–1072) wrote a scientifically informed treatise entitled "Luoyang mudan ji" 洛陽牡丹記 (Account of the tree peonies of Luoyang).[11] This work, written in approximately 1034, records that with the skill of gardeners, splendiferous peonies were crafted, and he mentions some of the more spectacular variants. In the treatise, Ouyang displays his practical knowledge of the botanical aspects of the flower's cultivation and hybridization. It seems that he had personally cultivated the peony, giving a suggestion or two for how to graft stalks and the methods for preparing the soil to raise seeds.[12]

While Ouyang Xiu at times succumbs to the beauty of the peony, he, along with other writers, displays an ambivalent stance on its nature.[13] In the first section, he acknowledges that the peony is a "concentration of beauty" but asserts also that it is also an "anomalous growth" (*yao* 妖), a result of the earth going against (*fan* 反) objects.[14] This might be one of the earliest recorded stances against modified organisms. Nonetheless, Ouyang Xiu provides a list of the twenty-four famous Luoyang peony species and cultigens, and admits that his inventory is incomplete.

In spite of his misgivings, Ouyang Xiu collected paintings of peonies as well. According to an anecdote recorded by the Song-dynasty intellect Shen Kuo 沈括 (1031–1095), who was an acquaintance of Ouyang Xiu's, they discussed the skills of two painters who, among other subject matter, also depicted flowers, Xu Xi 徐熙 (d. before 975) and Huang Quan 黃筌 (c. 903–965).[15]

Ouyang Xiu once obtained an old painting of a clump of peonies beneath which was a cat (*li*), but was uncertain of its merits. The minister Wu Yu [1004–1058] who was related to Ouyang by marriage, as soon as he saw it, said: "These are peonies at mid-day. How do I know this? The flowers are wide open and their colors are dry; these are the flowers of the middle of the day. The cat's eye have thread-like black pupils; these are a cat's eyes at mid-day. Flowers with dew on them have closely gathered petals and their colors are moist. A cat's eyes have round pupils in the morning and evening, but during the day they gradually narrow and lengthen, so that by mid-day they are just like a thread."[16]

Shen Kuo's description of the paintings brings us back to *Calico Cat under Peonies*. His passage endorses a highly naturalistic mode of representation. Through closely looking at the phenomena—peonies and cats—Wu Yu apprehends their natural responses to their environment in a moment of time. Onlookers may gain knowledge of nature or of paintings and their meanings after observing things closely and in minute detail. From Wu Yu's precise description of the cat's pupils as presented in Shen Kuo's account, we can also know that there was more than one cat-with-peony painting. The eyes of the feline in *Calico Cat with Peonies* are not depicted with thread-like pupils, but consist of round circular dots; if Wu Yu is correct, the time of this painting is either morning or evening. The artist of another painting, presumably very similar to *Calico Cat with Peonies*, sought to create imagery displaying skillful brushwork that captured lifelike resemblances.

Shen Kuo's comments, perhaps appealing to discerning members of the educated elite, discuss peonies in terms other than their beauty or associations with wealth and nobility. Shen Kuo's account and Wu Yu's discussion address the appearance of the peonies in their natural state at midday, opened wide without dewy coloring, looking beyond their glamorous qualities.[17] But the auspicious sentiments remained important for other consumers of peonies and their representations. The *Xuanhe Hua Pu* 宣和畫譜, or *Catalogue of Paintings in the Xuanhe Imperial Collections*, of circa 1120 explicitly states that artists should invoke qualities of wealth and aristocracy when painting peonies: "Therefore, [in depicting] tree peonies and herbaceous peonies, as well as phoenixes and peacocks, [the painter] must bring out their wealthy and aristocratic [qualities]" 故花之於牡丹芍藥, 禽之於鸞鳳孔翠, 必使之富貴。[18] These connections between the peony, prosperity, and nobility draw upon the history of the peony and strive to consolidate its premiere status in the kingdom of flowers. The prestige Shu Yuanyu granted to the top-ranking peony was reaffirmed centuries later.

Conclusions

The peony's unending ability to display ethereal beauty continued to captivate aficionados who treasured its vibrant colors and exquisite blooms, with or without thousands of petals. In *Peonies and Butterfly*, a painting formerly attributed to Qian Xuan 錢選 (1239–1301), presently mounted as a hanging scroll, peonies are

Peonies and a Butterfly
© 2020 Museum of Fine Arts, Boston.

depicted provocatively, splaying their splendid plethora of petals for all to admire. The painting, dating to the late thirteenth century, represents the peony cherished as a hybridized beauty, reinforcing claims to social status and wealth. The peonies are painted with great precision, participating in the joy of observing the object and reproducing its exuberant beauty. The beauty of the peony reigns supreme. In the following centuries in China and beyond, the elegant peony graces many a surface, including silk, paper, porcelain, and fabric, bringing the exquisite bloom from the garden for all to behold and to admire.

The Peony Emboldened

Inspired Visions of Floral Fortitude at the University of Michigan Museum of Art

Rosalyn L. Hammers

Who is able to resist the ravishing beauty of the peony? All may be smitten, but some artists and artisans have moved beyond the allure of the peony to celebrate other qualities it displays. In these images the peony has inspired artists to contemplate its strength and vigor, investigating the ways in which the flower nurtures and sustains its gorgeous blooms. When the peony is represented in monochromatic formal qualities, the blossom is still gorgeous, but artists may seek to explore other qualities of the flower. In a variety of media, artists acknowledge the beauty of the peony, but represent the plant with flourish and innovation, encouraging viewers to see additional aspects of the peony that are not simply about their sumptuous blooms.

Artists such as Yong-chin Kim and Kumashiro Yūhi may emphasize the fortitude they see in the peony, depicting the vital tenacity with which the flower propels its blossoms outward. The blossoms are beautiful, but the force of nature that makes the bloom possible itself is celebrated in these artists' interpretations. Peonies are often depicted with a sense of self-possession, a floral beauty bursting with self-confidence. The photographer John Dugdale challenges the ease and tranquility of the flower in *Cornwall Peonies*. At least seven blossoms, wind and rain swept, are arranged as a cluster and in disarray. It appears that the blooms are on the same bush, with the petals of the flower in the viewer's lower right, out of focus and in motion. This photo, an albumen silver print in monochromatic sepia, evokes the past, and the passing quality of time, even for peonies. Through framing, the arched composition underscores the decisions the artist has made to contain the blooms within his vision. Dugdale's representation of peonies explores a sense of vulnerability,

Above: Pink and turquoise jacket with appliqué and key design, China, 19th century, applique and embroidery on silk. University of Michigan Museum of Art, gift of Mr. and Mrs. Herbert W. Johe, 1989/2.70.

Right: Cosmetic box with inlaid peony design, Korea, Goryeo dynasty (918–1392), late 12th century, stoneware with inlaid decoration under celadon glaze. University of Michigan Museum of Art, gift of Bruce and Inta Hasenkamp and museum purchase made possible by Elder and Mrs. Sang-Yong Nam, 2004/1.240A&B.

Preceding page: Kim Yongjin (Korea, 1878–1968), *Flowers* (detail), 1946, album leaves, ink and color on paper. University of Michigan Museum of Art, museum purchase, 1952/2.5.

but at the same affirms their tremulous strength to withstand both environment and time.

Other artists and artisans have represented the peony with its bright colors to emblazon handscrolls and clothing. The Chinese artist Ma Yuanyu depicted the blossom as a whorling pile of pink petals that rotates outward to greet the viewer. In the pink and turquoise jacket with appliqué and key design *(facing page, top)*, elegant stylized peonies punctuate the garment at the shoulder closure and waist, floral beauties that enhanced the vivacious quality of the wearer.

The peony enlivens the surfaces of stoneware and porcelain objects. In the twelfth-century Korean cosmetic box *(facing page, bottom)*, the peony is inlaid onto the surface of the vessel with white clay. After an application of celadon glaze, the stoneware clay dish was fired in a kiln, and gained a semi-glossy appearance. The drawing of the peony across the cosmetic box emphasizes dynamic and rhythmic lines to suggest the vitality of the peony as it springs up from the earth. Blossoms, poised on a coiled stem, are centered within an entourage of leaves. Within a circular composition, the vivacious peony radiates forth, extending vitality through curvaceous lines.

Bottom left: John Dugdale (b.1960), *Cornwall Peonies*, 2002, albumen silver print. University of Michigan Museum of Art, museum purchase made possible by the Harry Denham Trust, 2003/1.380.

Bottom right: Plate with blue-and-white willow, peony, and bridge design, China, Qing dynasty (1644–1912), late 19th century, porcelain with blue underglaze painting. University of Michigan Museum of Art, gift of the William T. and Dora G. Hunter Collection, UA2002.30.

The Peony Emboldened

Kumashiro Yūhi (Japan, 1713–1772), *Peonies and Rock*, Edo period (1615–1868), 18th century, hanging scroll, ink on paper. University of Michigan Museum of Art, museum purchase, Acquisition Fund, 1978/2.59.

The painted application of cobalt or copper blue pigment as an under glaze across a porcelain vessel's body likewise underscores the fortitude of the peony. The beast in the magnificent large serving plate with design of lion romping among peonies *(bottom, left)* leaps across a waterfall in a burgeoning scene of nature's abundance. The exuberant lion lands safely among the peonies skirt around the bottom edge of the plate.

The peony depicted in the center of plate with blue-and-white willow, peony and bridge design *(previous page, bottom right)* is whimsically gigantic. This peony is featured with a willow, and this alludes to a popular theme familiar to aficionados of blue and white porcelain. The Willow pattern, also referred to as the Blue Willow, was created in eighteenth-century England, by drawing upon motifs found in imported Chinese porcelain. It traditionally represented a garden scene with a bridge, pagodas, flying birds, and willow trees. As the theme gained popularity in Europe, Chinese artists received commissions to produce sets of porcelain dinnerware with this pattern. The artist of this plate was emboldened by the beauty of the peony, and painted it in a scale larger than life. In addition the flower is depicted four times along the edge of the plate. The peony's prominence in this design challenges the privileged position of the willow, standing as inspiring testimony to the great vitality and fortitude of the flower.

Above: Ma Yuanyu (China, ca. 1669–1722), *Flowers* (detail), Qing dynasty (1644–1912), late 17th–early 18th century, handscroll, ink and color on paper. University of Michigan Museum of Art, gift of Mr. H.C. Weng, 1966/2.36.

Left: Large serving plate with design of lion romping among peonies, Japan, Meiji era (1868–1912), late 19th century, porcelain with blue and black underglaze painting. University of Michigan Museum of Art, gift of Mr. and Mrs. Richard M. Cook, 1969/1.83.

Notes

A Century of Blooms

1. Martha Gilmore Parfet and Corcoran, Mary B. 2014. *Keep the Quality Up: The Story of the Upjohn & Gilmore, Van Zant & Parfet Families.* pp. 146–47.

2. Sally Linvill Bund. "The Life of Aubrey William Tealdi and His Design of the Estate Grounds of Arnold H. and Gertrude E. Goss," unpublished paper, Dec. 9, 1992.

3. Wilhelm Miller. 1915. *The Prairie Spirit in Landscape Gardening.* Urbana, IL: Agricultural Experiment Station, Department of Horticulture, University of Illinois. Circular #184; Robert E. Grese. 2000. Introduction to *Landscape Gardening,* by Ossian Cole Simonds, Amherst: University of Massachusetts Press. p. xx.

4. University of Michigan, Board of Regents. *Proceedings of the Board of Regents* (1920–23), 715.

5. Bund, "The Life of Aubrey William Tealdi."

6. Aubrey Tealdi, "Peony Garden at Ann Arbor," *American Peony Society Bulletin* 21, no. 39 (September 1929): 3–7.

7. Aubrey Tealdi. Landscape Design Lecture, June 6, 1924. Unpublished paper, p. 3.

8. "Ann Arbor Peony Time Arrives: Thousands of Flowers in Now Bloom," *Ann Arbor News*, 13 June 1935.

9. "Ann Arbor Peony Time Arrives."

10. "Variety of Color Features Peony Exhibition at Nichols Arboretum," *Ann Arbor News*, 17 June 1927.

11. "Variety of Color Features Peony Exhibition at Nichols Arboretum."

12. "Ann Arbor Peony Time Arrives."

13. Virginia Ford. 2017. *Ginger Stands Her Ground.* Ann Arbor, MI: Ann Arbor District Library. pp. 40–41.

14. University of Michigan, Proceedings of the Board of Regents, (1920–23), 578. https://quod.lib.umich.edu/u/umregproc/acw7513.1920.001/678?page=root; size=100;view=image. https://quod.lib.umich.edu/u/umregproc/acw7513.1926.001/00000313?page=root;size=100;view=image

15. Tealdi, "Peony Garden at Ann Arbor."

16. University of Michigan, Proceedings of the Board of Regents, (1926–29), 239.

17. Aubrey Tealdi, "Peony Garden at Ann Arbor"; Aubrey Tealdi, "The Nichols Arboretum," *American Peony Society Bulletin* 21, no. 46 (June 1931): 25–28.

Brook Lodge Gardens—Peonies

1. Early in the twentieth century the American Peony Society developed a ten-point scoring system to compare and rank peony flowers for relative perfection. The formal rating ended in the 1930s. Upjohn was an active point-scorer, and the quest for excellence was important to him.

Silvia Saunders

1. Extensive documentation at Winterthur was organized and summarized by Valencia Libby, research associate in garden history. All quotations about peonies at Winterthur, the Chelsea Flower Show, and the activities of H. F. du Pont are from her meticulous files.

2. A profile of genomic research using Saunders's peonies in the Root Garden at Hamilton College: https://www.hamilton.edu/arboretum/root-glen/root-glen-history

3. Christian Goodwillie, director and curator of Special Collections at Hamilton College, and his colleague Katherine Collette provided exceptional assistance in tracking down field notebooks of Professor Saunders as well as Silvia Saunders's images.

4. Bill Seidl's interactions with Silvia Saunders are from *Seidl's Life with Peonies* of 12 December 2017, posted by the Peony Society, www.peonysociety.eu

5. Joan Lee Faust's Around the Garden column in the 2 June 1974 *New York Times* captures a sense of Silvia Saunders's challenge to the gardening public.

Edward Auten Jr.

1. Auten introduced only a few peonies bred by others but named by him—these are included in the 297 count. An additional set were bred by him but subsequently named and introduced by the Gilbert Wild & Son Nursery of Missouri. The combined set accounts for various statements that he bred or introduced more than three hundred peonies.

2. All Auten quotations are from his catalogs of 1926–34.

3. Harvard graduation program and Harvard secretary reports from updates at five and ten years after graduation. Auten was a classmate of (future) President F. D. Roosevelt, of whom he had pithy observations. These and other recollections about Auten from community members who worked for him as school children are being compiled in community archives in Princeville.

4. Obituary in the *Princeville Telephone*, 16 May 1974.

5. F. F. Weinard and Herman B. Dorner, *Peonies: Single and Japanese in the Illinois Trial Garden* (Urbana: University of Illinois Agricultural Experiment Station, 1938). Internet resource.

6. See Michener and Vlasava's "Conserving Beauty as Science" in this volume.

7. See the entry for 'Chocolate Soldier' in David C. Michener and Carol A. Adelman, *Peony: The Best Varieties for Your Garden* (Portland, OR: Timber Press, 2017). A historic theater trailer of "The Chocolate Soldier" (all-white cast) is https://www.youtube.com/watch?v=H9K8f7ilaOY

Mrs. Sarah A. Pleas

1. Lee R. Bonnewitz, *Jubilee at the Reading Peony Show*, 2nd ed. (Van Wert, OH: privately published, 1920).

2. "Why Is the Peony Queen called Queen Jubilee?," *Van Wert Tricounty Ledger*, 24 April 2016.

3. See "Historic Peonies in Early America," by Peggy Cornett, in this volume.

4. *Peonies for Pleasure*, 5th ed. (Springfield, OH: Good & Reese Co., n.d.), 6. https://archive.org/stream/CAT31305691/CAT31305691_djvu.txt

5. W. E. Upjohn, *Brook Lodge Gardens—Peonies* (Kalamazoo, MI: privately published, undated but internal evidence is circa 1924).

6. AT 90 SHE GROWS PEONIES: MRS. PLEAS'S BLOSSOMS ADMIRED AT SHOW JUST CLOSED HERE. (1916, June 12). *New York Times (1857-1922)*. https://proxy.lib.umich.edu/login?url=https://search.proquest.com/docview/97919676?accountid=14667

7. See "Conserving Beauty as Science," by Michener and Vlasava, in this volume.

Amateur Breeders and Peony Enthusiasts

1. Grace Shackman, "When Downtown Was Hardware Heaven," *Ann Arbor Observer,* May 1994. https://aadl.org/aaobserver/18216

2. "Personal," *Ann Arbor News*, 10 June 1921.

3. Grace Shackman, "Weinberg's Peony Garden," *Ann Arbor Observer*, June 1984. https://aadl.org/aaobserver/13031

4. "Ann Arbor Peony Growers Honored," *Ann Arbor News*, 19 June 1935.

5. "Ann Arbor Peony Growers Honored."

The Peony Garden at Fair Lane

1. "Fair Lane, the House and Gardens," Ford Motor Company Archives Bulletin No. 3, Henry Ford Collections, Dearborn, Michigan, 1955.

2. Keith Clark, "The Reminiscences of Mr. Alfons De Caluwe," March 1952, Oral History Section, Ford Motor Company Archives, Henry Ford Collections, Dearborn, Michigan.

3. W. Ormiston Roy, Landscape Gardener, Henry Ford Collections, Dearborn, Michigan, Acc. 1, Box 42, Letter to Clara B. Ford, 29 July 1928.

4. Handwritten order list on the back side of correspondence from Edward Auten Jr. to Clara B. Ford, Henry Ford Collections, Dearborn, Michigan, Acc. 1, Box 42, 29 September 1927.

5. Doris Guidry, Assistant Director, Fair Lane Conference Center, Fair Lane Archives, Dearborn, Michigan, Letter to Mrs. C. R. Johnson (Garden Club of Dearborn), 18 November 1982.

Historic Peonies in Early America

1. Alice Morse Earle, *Old Time Gardens: Newly Set Forth* (New York: Macmillan, 1901), 42.
2. Edward Sprague Rand Jr., *Popular Flowers, and How to Cultivate Them* (Boston: Shepart and Gill, 1873), 96.
3. Louise Beebe Wilder, *Colour in My Garden* (Garden City, NY: Doubleday, Page, 1918), 119.
4. Joseph Breck, *The Flower-Garden; or, Breck's Book of Flowers* (Boston: John P. Jewett, 1851), 69.

Conserving Beauty as Science

1. GeneBank is the genetic sequence database of all known DNA sequences made available to the public by the US National Institutes of Health. https://www.ncbi.nlm.nih.gov/genbank/

From The Book of the Peony

1. Iliad, 5, 401, etc. Another apparent instance of the peony's efficacy as a cure for wounds is also given in the Iliad (5, 899, etc.). "So spake he (Jove) and bade Paeon heal him (Mars). And Paeon laid assuaging drugs upon the wounds and healed him seeing he was in no wise of mortal mould. Even as fig juice rapidly thickens white milk that is liquid before but curdleth while one stirreth it, even so swiftly healed he impetuous Mars."
2. The Latin name Paeonia is the feminine of Paeonius—"belonging to Paeon."
3. Liddell & Scott, Greek-English Lexicon (1888), p. 1106.
4. Natural History: Book XXV, Ch. 10.
5. Natural History: Book XXV, Ch. 60.

The Peony in Painting and Verse in China from the Eighth to the Thirteenth Centuries

1. Lin Lina 林莉娜, "Fu gui hua li" 富貴花狸 *Calico Cat under Peonies*, in *Da Guan: Bei Song shu hua te zhan* 大觀:北宋書特展 [Grand view: Special exhibition of Northern Sung painting and calligraphy] (Taipei: Guo li gu gong bo wu yuan, 2006), 207–9.
2. 遨遊之士如狂焉, 亦上國繁華之一事也。My translation with assistance from Ruby Leung Pui Yi. Source of Chinese is "Mudan fu" 牡丹賦 [Rhapsody of peonies], in *Zhongguo mu dan: Pei yu yu jian shang ji wen hua yuan yuan* 中國牡丹: 培育與鑒賞及文化淵源 [The peonies of China: Cultivation, appreciation, and cultural origins], ed. Wang Gaochao 王高潮 and Liu Zhongjian 劉仲健 (Beijing: Zhongguo lin ye chu ban she, 2000) front matter, n.p.
3. This poem is in the form of a *yong wu ci* 詠物詞, or "song lyrics on objects," a genre in which a poet offers lyrical expression to observed entities and phenomena in the material world. Lin Shuen-fu, *The Transformation of the Chinese Lyrical Tradition: Chiang K'uei and the Southern Sung Tz'u Poetry* (Princeton, NJ: Princeton University Press, 1978), 10.

4. The tomb had been robbed before researchers discovered it. Cultural Relics Research Institute of Hebei province, *Wu dai Wang Chuzhi mu* 五代王處直墓 (The tomb of Wang Chuzhi of the Five Dynasties) (Beijing: Wen wu chu ban she, 1998).

5. The famous poet Tang poet Bai Juyi 白居易 (772–846) valued these kinds of stones because they had experienced great forces that had profound impact on their forms.

A Pair of Rocks 雙石 *by Bai Juyi* 白居易 *(772–846)*
Dark sallow, two slates of rocks,
Their appearance is grotesque and ugly.
Of vulgar use they are incapable;
People of the time detest and abandon them.
Molded into their current shapes from their primordial cast,
I got them at the mouth of Lake Dongting;
For ten thousand years they had been left at the water bank;
Then all of a sudden they fell into my hands.
. . . .
Each man has his own penchant;
All things seek their own companions.
I am beginning to feel that the world of youngsters
Would not accommodate a man with drooping white hair.
Turning my head around, I ask the pair of rocks:
"Can you keep company with an old man like myself?"
Although the rocks cannot speak,
They promise that we will be three friends.
蒼然兩片石, 厥狀怪且醜。俗用無所堪, 時人嫌不取。
結從胚渾始, 得自洞庭口。萬古遺水濱, 一朝入吾手 . . .
人皆有所好, 物各求其偶。漸恐少年場, 不容垂白叟。
回頭問雙石, 能伴老夫否。石雖不能言, 許我為三友。

Bai Juyi as quoted by Yang Xiaoshan, *Metamorphosis of the Private Sphere: Gardens and Objects in Tang-Song Poetry* (Cambridge, MA: Harvard University Press, 2003), 100.

6. Tonia Eckfield, *Imperial Tombs in Tang China, 618–907: The Politics of Paradise* (London: RoutledgeCurzon, 2005).

7. The dates for Li Jun are problematic, but Denis C. Twitchett has assigned him to the ninth century. Li Jun, however, at times is recorded as active in the eighth century. Denis C. Twitchett, *The Writing of Official History under the T'ang* (Cambridge: Cambridge University Press, 1992), 43.

8. Li Bai as translated by Paula M. Varsona, *Tracking the Banished Immortal: The Poetry of Li Bo and Its Critical Reception* (Honolulu: University of Hawai'i Press, 2003), 246. For a discussion of Li Bai's poem, see pp. 245–56. My interpretation of the poem relies to a great extent on her observations.

9. Yang Guifei nearly cost the emperor his kingdom, and the people of the Tang their dynasty. Because Emperor Xuanzong was so enchanted by her beauty, he neglected affairs of the state, and rebellion resulted. He, along with Yang, fled from the capital with followers and military support. In the foreboding mountains of what is present-day Sichuan province, the generals threatened to withdraw their

allegiance if the emperor continued to dally with Yang. They issued an ultimatum: either the generals or Yang Guifei had to go. She was hanged from a tree.

10. Buying Flowers　　買花

帝城春欲暮	*A spring nears its end in the imperial city*
喧喧車馬度	*A clamor of carriages and horses passes by.*
共道牡丹時	*Everyone says it is peony season*
相隨買花去	*They hurry after each other to buy the flowers.*
貴賤無常價	*Expensive or cheap, there is no set price,*
酬直看花數	*The cost depends on the size of the blossom.*
灼灼百朵紅	*Gleaming, a hundred pearls of crimson,*
戔戔五束素	*Closely layered, five sprays of white.*
上張帷幕庇	*Canopies are spread overhead to shade them,*
旁織巴籬護	*Bamboo fences protect them on the side.*
水灑復泥封	*They are sprinkled with water and packed in mud,*
移來色如故	*So transplanting does not harm their appearance.*
家家習為俗	*Every household takes part in the festivities,*
人人迷不悟	*Every person is caught up in the delusion.*
有一田舍翁	*An old man of farming stock*
偶來買花處	*Happened to pass by the flower market.*
低頭獨長嘆	*He lowered his eye and heaved a long sigh,*
此嘆無人⊠	*A sigh no one understood.*
一叢深色花	*"One cluster of deeply colored blossoms*
十戶中人賦	*Would pay the taxes of ten ordinary households."*

Bai Juyi as translated, with slight modification, by Ronald Egan, *The Problem of Beauty: Aesthetic Thought and Pursuits in Northern Song Dynasty China* (Cambridge, MA: Harvard University Asia Center, Harvard University Press, 2006), 112–13.

11. Scientific knowledge here is to be understood as the formation of knowledge and inquiry about the world through observation and study, based on the Latin term *scire*, to know. In this essay science is a heuristic device, and not the historical construction of science as initiated in eighteenth- or nineteenth-century Europe.

12. Egan, *Problem of Beauty*, 115–17.

13. Egan, *Problem of Beauty*, 121–29.

14. Ouyang Xiu as translated by Egan, *Problem of Beauty*, 119. From section 1 of Ouyang Xiu's "Treatise on the Tree Peony," 已凡物不常有而為害乎人者曰災, 不常有而徒可怪駭不為害者曰妖, 語曰：天反時為災, 地反物為妖, 此亦草木之妖, 而萬物之一怪也。然比夫癭木癰腫者竊獨鍾其美, 而見幸於人焉。"

15. Susan Bush and Hsio-yen Shih, *Early Chinese Texts on Painting* (Cambridge, MA: Harvard University Press, 1985), 126–27.

16. Shen Kuo as translated by Bush and Shih, *Early Chinese Texts on Painting*, with changes from Wades-Giles to Pinyin romanization, 123. 歐陽公嘗得一古畫牡丹叢, 其下有一貓, 未知其精粗。丞相正肅吳公與歐公姻家, 一見曰：「此『正午牡丹』也。何以明之。其花披哆而色燥, 此日中時花也。貓眼黑睛如線, 此正午貓眼也。有帶露花, 則房斂而色澤。貓眼早暮則睛圓, 日漸中狹長, 正午則如一線耳。」。

17. The art historian Maggie Bickford has traced the rise of the plum blossom during the twelfth century, arguing that this flower supplanted the peony,

particularly among the scholarly elite. Maggie Bickford, *Ink Plum: The Making of a Chinese Scholar-Painting Genre* (Cambridge: Cambridge University Press, 1996).

18. Author's translation in consultation with those of Bickford, *Ink Plum*, 105; and Bush and Shih, *Early Chinese Texts on Painting*, 128. Chinese is from *Xuanhe Huapu* 宣和畫譜 (Imperial catalog of the Xuanhe era) in *Hua shi cong shu* 畫史叢書 (Compendium of texts on the history of painting), ed. Yu Anlan 于安瀾 (Shanghai: Shanghai ren min mei shu chu ban she, 1963), vol. 2, *juan* 15, p. 163.

Contributors

Carol A. Adelman is co-owner of Adelman Peony Gardens in Brooks, Oregon. She is the coauthor of *Peony: The Best Varieties for Your Garden* (Timber Press, 2017). Carol is a member of the Board of Directors of the American Peony Society. She is on the Peony Garden's Advisory Committee.

Stephane Bailleul is Botaniste in the division recherché et development scientifique at the Jardin botanique de Montreal, Quebec, Canada.

Harvey Buchite co-owns Hidden Springs Flower Farm in Spring Grove, Minnesota, where he and his wife grow over six hundred peonies. He is past president and member of the board of directors of the American Peony Society and the Minnesota Peony Society. He is on the Peony Garden's Advisory Committee.

Peggy Cornett is Co-director of Monticello and its Thomas Jefferson Center for Historic Plants. She is also Co-director of the Historic Landscape Institute and oversees educational programs at Monticello. She is on the Peony Garden's Advisory Committee.

Adrian Feng operates Southern Peony—a resource for growing peonies in the South (http://www.southernpeony.com/) and is a member of the board of directors of the American Peony Society.

Bethany Gosewehr is the Vice President of development at the Benjamin Harrison Presidential Site.

Robert Grese is a Professor of landscape architecture in the School for Environment and Sustainability at the University of Michigan as well as Director of the Matthaei Botanical Gardens and Nichols Arboretum. He is the author of *Jens Jensen: Maker of Natural Parks and Gardens* and *The Native Landscape Reader*.

Roslyn L. Hammers, an Associate Professor of art history at the University of Hong Kong, is a specialist in scientifically-informed imagery of China.

Alex Henderson is Curator of Living Collections at the Royal Botanical Gardens, Ontario, Canada.

Don Hollingsworth is a past President of the American Peony Society, where he has been a member for over fifty years. He is a peony nurseryman who operated Hollingsworth Peonies 1992–2012 and is an acclaimed breeder of new cultivars. He is on the Peony Garden's Advisory Committee.

Nina Koziol is a garden writer in the Chicago area and teaches garden design and horticulture classes at the Chicago Botanic Garden and the Morton Arboretum. Her website, www.thisgardencooks.com, provides advice for new and experienced gardeners.

Scott Kunst is the founder of Old House Gardens, a mail-order source for heirloom flower bulbs. He has taught landscape history at Eastern Michigan University. He is a member of our Peony Garden Advisory Committee.

Karen Marzonie is Director of Landscapes at Fair Lane, the home of Clara and Henry Ford in Dearborn, Michigan.

David Michener is Curator at the University of Michigan's Matthaei Botanical Gardens and Nichols Arboretum. He is coauthor (with Carol A. Adelman) of *Peony: The Best Varieties for Your Garden*.

Natsu Oyobe is Curator of Asian Art at the University of Michigan's Museum of Art.

David Stevenson is the Curator of Plant Collections at the Minnesota Landscape Arboretum.

Nastassia Vlasava is a Lead Researcher at the Central Botanical Gardens, National Academy of Sciences of Belarus, and an invited academic affiliate at the University of Michigan Matthaei Botanical Gardens and Nichols Arboretum.

Darren Wheimbecker is the owner, designer, and builder of Whistling Gardens in Wilsonville, Ontario, Canada.

Acknowledgments

We owe a debt of gratitude to the following individuals and organizations for their help with this book and the Peony Garden over recent years:

- The Peony Garden began in 1922 with a generous gift of plants from Dr. W. E. Upjohn, founder of the Upjohn Pharmaceutical Company of Kalamazoo, Michigan. Generous gifts from donors and members—and grants from the Stanley Smith Horticultural Trust and the Institute for Museum and Library Services have made the Peony Garden initiative possible

- Special thanks to the families of W. E. Upjohn, Philip and Kathy Power, Ian and Sally Bund, Smilka Zdravkovska, and the Porter Family Foundation

- Academician Vladimir V. Titok, Director, and the staff of the Central Botanical Gardens, National Academy of Sciences of Belarus for ongoing projects and support

- Photographers Wil Brinkerhoff, Oscar Brubaker, Julia Lawson, Larry Miller, Scott Soderberg, Michele Yanga, and many others whose photographs grace these pages

- Janet Kohler and the *Ann Arbor Observer* for contributing artwork and assisting with our outreach into the Ann Arbor community. www.janetkohlerarts.com

- Grace Shackman and Susan Wineberg for their help in researching local history

- The late Linda Cody who helped us articulate a vision for renovating the Peony Garden

- Members of our Peony Garden Advisory Board who contributed critical advice and support both for the renovation of the garden as well as for this book: Carol Adelman, Harvey Buchite, Peggy Cornett, Lindsay D'Aoust, Don Hollingsworth, Jeff Jabco, Reiner Jacobowski, Scott Kunst, Scott Parker, Don Smith, and Jim Waddick

- Peter Olin who provided a critical review of the Peony Garden as part of the Plant Collections Network through the American Public Gardens Association

- The board members of the American Peony Society whose expertise and photographs contributed to the richness of peonies depicted here

- Ann Arbor Farm & Garden

- Dr. Vladimir V. Titok, Academician Vladimir N. Reshetnikov, and the staff of the Central Botanical Gardens, National Academy of Sciences of Belarus for the ongoing projects and support

- Our many staff members and volunteers from Matthaei Botanical Gardens and Nichols Arboretum who have helped make the Peony Garden a special place for the University of Michigan and broader community

- Scott Ham, Paula Newcomb, Mary Hashman, and others at the University of Michigan Press for all of their creative efforts and patience with us to make this book a reality

What's with the Ants?

You don't have to be around peonies for long before realizing that ants love these plants. Woe to the person who brings cut peony flowers inside the house without first addressing the ants.

Why do peonies attract ants? Legend has frequently been that the ants help peonies flowers to bloom. There's no evidence for that, but peonies do have a beneficial relationship with ants. Peony flowers have extrafloral nectaries around the bud that secrete a sugary substance that attracts ants. Ants will climb the flower stem, feed on the sugary substance and move on to the next flower. Along the way, they leave a pheromone trail that attracts other ants to the available feast. As for benefiting the peonies, the ants may devour other insects they find, or their simple presence may act to deter other insects. They're a bit like a preventive force, warding off other more harmful predators. If you've noticed, peonies as a group seem to have very few insect pests. So, the next time you see ants crawling around the peony plants you enjoy, thank them for helping to protect these valued flowers!